PUSH

JEWELRY

PUSH

JEWELRY

30 Artists Explore the Boundaries of Jewelry

Curated by Arthur Hash

LARK CRAFTS
Asheville

EDITOR
MARTHE LE VAN

EDITORIAL ASSISTANCE
ABBY HAFFELT
HANNAH DOYLE

ART DIRECTOR &
COVER DESIGNER
KATHLEEN HOLMES

ART PRODUCTION
KAY HOLMES STAFFORD

JUNIOR DESIGNER
CAROL BARNAO

FRONT COVER
Mirjam Hiller
Ovalias Brooch, 2010

PAGE 2
Susanne Klemm
Greenwood—Rings, 2011

FACING PAGE
Julia deVille
Trophy Mouse Brooch, 2006

BACK COVER, TOP LEFT
Laura Deakin
Hidden Pearls, 2007

BACK COVER, TOP RIGHT
Robean Visschers
Pink Ring, 2009

BACK COVER, MIDDLE LEFT
Carolina Gimeno
*From Series III: Draw the Mist—
Pendant, 2010*

BACK COVER, MIDDLE RIGHT
Beppe Kessler
One Night, 2009

BACK COVER, BOTTOM LEFT
Joe Wood
T-V Bracelet 3, 2007

BACK COVER, BOTTOM RIGHT
Lucy Sarneel
A Touch of Magic II, 2011

LARK CRAFTS

An Imprint of Sterling Publishing
387 Park Avenue South
New York, NY 10016

If you have questions or comments about
this book, please visit: larkcrafts.com

Library of Congress Cataloging-in-Publication Data

PUSH jewelry : 30 Artists Explore the Boundaries of
Jewelry / editor, Marthe Le Van. -- First Edition.
    pages cm
  ISBN 978-1-4547-0368-6 (hardback)
  1. Artist-designed jewelry--History--21st century--
Themes, motives. I. Le Van, Marthe, editor.
  NK7310.5.P87 2012
  739.2709'051--dc23

                                    2012001046

10 9 8 7 6 5 4 3 2 1

First Edition

Published by Lark Crafts
An Imprint of Sterling Publishing Co., Inc.
387 Park Avenue South, New York, NY 10016

Text © 2012, Lark Crafts, an Imprint of
Sterling Publishing Co., Inc.
Photography © 2012, Artist/Photographer

Distributed in Canada by Sterling Publishing,
c/o Canadian Manda Group, 165 Dufferin Street
Toronto, Ontario, Canada M6K 3H6

Distributed in the United Kingdom by GMC Distribution
Services, Castle Place, 166 High Street, Lewes, East
Sussex, England BN7 1XU

Distributed in Australia by Capricorn Link (Australia)
Pty Ltd., P.O. Box 704, Windsor, NSW 2756 Australia

Manufactured in China

ISBN 13: 978-1-4547-0368-6

For information about custom editions, special
sales, and premium and corporate purchases,
please contact the Sterling Special Sales
Department at specialsales@sterlingpub.com or
800-805-5489.

Requests for information about desk and
examination copies available to college and
university professors must be submitted to
academic@larkbooks.com. Our complete policy
can be found at www.larkcrafts.com.

10

16

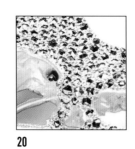

20

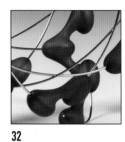

26

32

38

42

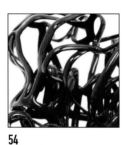

48

54

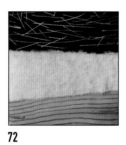

60

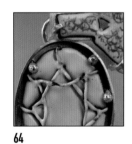

64

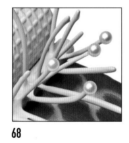

68

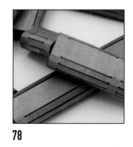

72

78

84

ENTS

Welcome to *PUSH*, an exciting book series exploring contemporary artists who "push" the boundaries of traditional design mediums. The 30 jewelers I selected for this book stretch the definition of jewelry by using exciting new materials, exploring innovative fabrication techniques, playing with historical references, and presenting the remarkable results as wearable art. Coming from spots across the globe, each one brings a signature aesthetic to this diverse collection.

Jewelry speaks to us in a variety of ways. It can be powerful and influential or peaceful and inviting. It can be shocking and offensive. Once a piece leaves an artist's hands, it connects with the body of the wearer to start a new life— one that's affected, at least, by the intentions of the artist. Jewelry is not merely decoration. It can serve as a shield, tell a story, or even indicate membership in a secret society.

As a jeweler and an educator, I'm interested in the whys and hows that lie behind a piece of jewelry. When I hold a handmade bracelet or brooch, so many questions spring to mind: What attracted the maker to a certain material? How would I wear the piece? Why is the piece a particular color? In the interviews that I conducted with the artists, I hoped to get at some of these questions, to explore the reasons why—the psychology behind the selections.

For a jeweler, each piece can create a whole new set of considerations the wearer may never consider. And vice versa. The reasons why someone chooses to wear a piece of jewelry—motivations like memory, emotion, and symbolism—can form a lengthy list. But the choice can also be very simple—a snap decision based on personal taste: "These earrings are red. I like red." Whether preference is driven by an instinctive reaction or a more deeply rooted rationale, jewelry always prompts a response. The one thing it rarely inspires is indifference.

As you flip through these pages, I hope you'll be as moved as I was by the work of artists who are balancing trends with traditions to lead the charge in contemporary jewelry design. The pieces they've created are some of the most exciting that I've seen in the past five years. Part of the undeniable pleasure of discovering these wonderful works was having the opportunity to interview the people who made them and to ask them important questions about the nature of their art.

The result of this inquiry is a book that allows you to peer into the mind of each artist. Collectively, this group represents a new breed of jewelry maker, one that isn't bound by material, value, or convention. They are creating a new language through their work. With *PUSH Jewelry*, I challenge you to forget what you think jewelry should be and consider what it can become.

Arthur Hash

ARTHUR HASH
UNITED STATES

"I use organic elements to create works that function as wearable pieces of adornment and as sculptural objects."

🔺 **UNTITLED**
2011 | Each: 4 x 4 x 3 cm
Paper, sterling silver
Photo by artist

GRASSLAND

2010 | 8 x 7 x 5 cm
Paper, paper clay, sterling silver
Photo by Hsiao-Chiao Juan

BLOSSOM II

2010 | 7 x 7 x 3.5 cm
Paper, paper clay, sterling silver
Photo by Hsiao-Chiao Juan

DESCRIBE YOUR WORK. I mix metalsmithing techniques with new technologies to create one-of-a-kind, wearable pieces and body adornments of paper and silver. The work is all about paper and layers—using multiple layers to create subtle movement and tactile qualities. **HOW HAS YOUR TECHNIQUE DEVELOPED?** During one period, I worked as a graphic designer and gained a lot of technical computer-design skills, which now help me a lot with jewelry design. At the Birmingham Institute of Art and Design in England, where I earned an MA in jewelry, I played with technologies such as 3D prototyping. The silversmithing skills that I gained from the university and from books now form the

UNTITLED ▶
2011 | Pendant: 2.5 x 2.5 x 1 cm
Paper, sterling silver
Photo by artist

◀ **LANDSCAPE II**
2010 | Each: 4 x 5 x 3.5 cm
Paper, paper clay, sterling silver
Photo by Hsiao-Chiao Juan

basic part of my work. **WHAT DO YOU LOVE ABOUT THE MATERIALS YOU USE?** I like the texture and the tactility that paper offers. It reveals itself through the work and always surprises me. I can layer it so that it gives my work an interactive functionality. **WHAT INSPIRES YOU THESE DAYS?** Natural forms, processes, and movements inspire me to make jewelry. I'm fascinated by the structure of organic forms. **WHAT RESPONSES DO YOU GET TO YOUR WORK?** People are fascinated by the

UNTITLED

2011 | Pendant: 4 x 4 x 1.7 cm
Paper, sterling silver
Photo by Mike Inch

MOUNTAIN LANDSCAPE II

2010 | 11 x 7 x 4 cm
Paper, paper clay, sterling silver
Photo by Hsiao-Chiao Juan

color of the pieces. They then look at my work more closely and are dazzled by the intricate paper patterns. The most common compliments I receive are "intricate, delicate, and unique." **HOW ARCHIVAL DO YOU CONSIDER YOUR WORK TO BE?** My work is archival in that it not only shows the value of the materials themselves, it also recreates the link

PEBBLES
2010 | Each: 2 x 6 x 5 cm
Paper, paper clay, sterling silver
Photo by Hsiao-Chiao Juan

UNTITLED

2011 | Pendant: 2.5 x 2.5 x 1 cm
Paper, sterling silver
Photo by artist

UNTITLED ▶

2011 | Pendant: 4 x 4 x 1 cm
Paper, sterling silver
Photo by Mike Inch

ALLYSON BONE

UNITED STATES

"By combining technology with traditional metalsmithing techniques, I create objects with a sense of history that still seem modern."

EARRINGS NO. 2 (MUSTACHE) ▶

2011 | Each: 4.2 x 3.4 x 0.6 cm
Sterling silver, onyx; fabricated, oxidized
Photo by artist

EARRINGS NO. 1 (GREEN EYES)

2011 | Each: 4 x 3.5 x 0.5 cm
Sterling silver, jade; fabricated, oxidized
Photo by artist

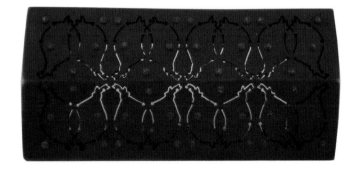

ONIONS

2009 | 2.6 x 6 x 1 cm
Sterling silver, stainless steel;
fabricated, hand pierced, oxidized
Photo by artist

PLENTY

2009 | 4 x 5.4 x 1.2 cm
Sterling silver, tourmaline, stainless steel;
fabricated, hand pierced, oxidized
Photo by artist

NECKLACE NO. 5 (PARTED LIPS)

2011 | 29 x 15 x 0.8 cm
Sterling silver, coral, nylon;
fabricated, oxidized
Photo by artist

PIERCED DAY/NIGHT EARRINGS

2008 | Each: 5.5 x 2 x 1.5 cm
Sterling silver; fabricated, hand pierced, oxidized
Photo by artist

NECKLACE NO. 6 (TWO LIDS)
2011 | 24 x 16 x 0.8 cm
Sterling silver, reconstructed onyx, nylon;
fabricated, oxidized
Photo by artist

PIERCED BROOCH #2
2008 | 6.5 x 7.5 x 1.6 cm
Sterling silver, stainless steel;
fabricated, hand pierced, oxidized
Photo by artist

"I consider

BIRD SHOULDER PIECE

2006 | 18 x 12 x 2 cm
Starling, gold leaf, black sapphires, leather; taxidermy
Photo by Terence Bogue

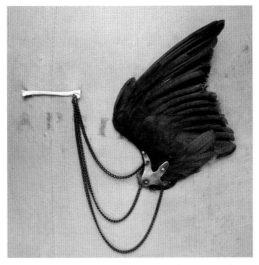

KINGFISHER WING BROOCH

2008 | 17 x 12 x 3 cm
Kingfisher wing, sterling silver; taxidermy, fabricated
Photo by Terence Bogue

SPARROW WING BROOCH

2010 | 14 x 11 x 1.5 cm
Sparrow wing, sterling silver; taxidermy, fabricated
Photo by Terence Bogue

DESCRIBE YOUR WORK. It's a combination of goldsmithing and silversmithing with materials that were once living—namely taxidermy animals. **HOW HAS YOUR TECHNIQUE DEVELOPED?** My pieces have grown larger over the years. Originally, I made brooches out of taxidermy animals, like small birds and mice. I slowly started working with bigger animals and now make sculptures out of taxidermy creatures adorned with my jewelry. **WHAT DO YOU LOVE ABOUT THE MATERIALS YOU USE?** I love the power and symbolism they carry. I see my materials as *memento mori*—reminders of mortality. I also believe the materials carry talismanic properties. **WALK ME THROUGH A DAY IN YOUR**

Q&A

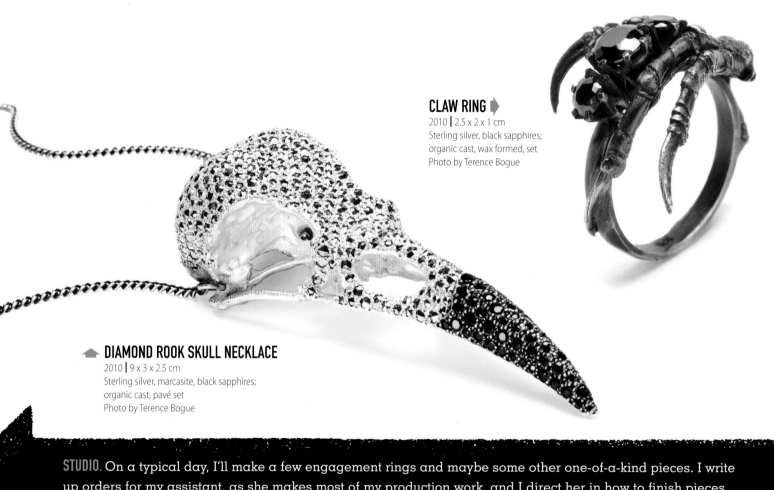

CLAW RING ▶
2010 | 2.5 x 2 x 1 cm
Sterling silver, black sapphires;
organic cast, wax formed, set
Photo by Terence Bogue

DIAMOND ROOK SKULL NECKLACE
2010 | 9 x 3 x 2.5 cm
Sterling silver, marcasite, black sapphires;
organic cast, pavé set
Photo by Terence Bogue

STUDIO. On a typical day, I'll make a few engagement rings and maybe some other one-of-a-kind pieces. I write up orders for my assistant, as she makes most of my production work, and I direct her in how to finish pieces, etc. Private clients often come by for consultations. If I'm close to an exhibition, I work 16-hour days, seven days a week. **WHAT INSPIRES YOU THESE DAYS?** The Memento Mori period—the fifteenth to the eighteenth centuries. Also: Victorian mourning jewelry, life, love, death, animals, and nature. **WHAT RESPONSES DO YOU GET TO YOUR WORK?** Overall, responses are very positive, but I get the odd person who is totally creeped out by dead things and can't come into my studio, which makes things difficult if he's after an engagement ring or a piece that doesn't involve

JET MOURNING BROOCH ▶
2004 | 4 x 2 x 1 cm
Jet, gold; carved, fabricated
Photos by Terence Bogue

taxidermy. I always find this funny, because the person is probably wearing a dead cow on his feet and probably eats animals, too! **SOME PEOPLE MIGHT FIND YOUR WORK REPULSIVE, BECAUSE YOU USE FOUND DEAD ANIMALS. DO YOU WANT PEOPLE TO WEAR YOUR WORK? DO YOU SEE CERTAIN PEOPLE WEARING CERTAIN PIECES?** I've only encountered a couple of people who have been repulsed by my work. Most people are curious about it, even if they wouldn't wear it. Buyers range from young goth kids to elderly conservative women. There are a lot of people who appreciate the taxidermy but don't feel brave enough to rock a dead mouse. So they'll get a different piece of mine, because they like the concepts

 ALEX LOUISE RING
2009 | 2.5 x 2 x 0.8 cm
18-karat white gold, diamonds, black
rhodium plating; wax formed, set
Photo by Terence Bogue

FUNERAL RING ▶
2011 | 3 x 2 x 1 cm
9-karat white gold, black rhodium
plating, garnet; wax formed,
fabricated, set, electroplated
Photo by Terence Bogue

TROPHY MOUSE BROOCH
2006 | 4.5 x 3.5 x 5 cm
Jet, mouse, gold; taxidermy, carved, fabricated
Photo by Terence Bogue

"A piece of jewelry is an area to zoom in on, a few centimeters of space with a high concentration of energy."

LA DOUBLE VIE

2009 | 42 x 2 x 2 cm
Zinc, paint, antique fabric, rubber, nylon thread; constructed, soldered, glued
Photo by Eric Knoote

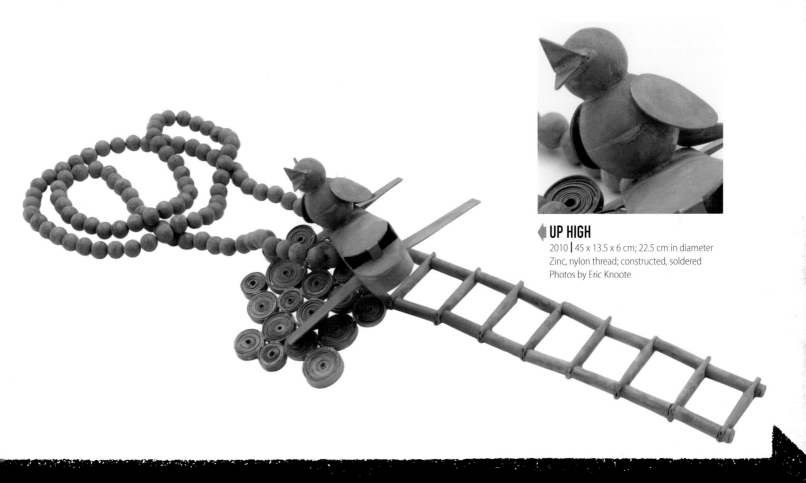

UP HIGH
2010 | 45 x 13.5 x 6 cm; 22.5 cm in diameter
Zinc, nylon thread; constructed, soldered
Photos by Eric Knoote

Q&A

DESCRIBE YOUR WORK. A blend of the mechanical and the organic, the manmade and the natural. It's sculptural, layered, and constructed of parts, which often results in a tension between simplicity and complexity. My work is imaginative in an abstract way, offering room for the observer to associate freely. **EARLY INFLUENCES?** Bathing in a zinc tub in the garden. Huge hydrangeas. Losing my first fake diamond ring with brilliant rainbow colors. From my fifth year on, I grew up in a little agricultural village in the south of the Netherlands. We had a garden full of plants and trees surrounded by meadows and a little forest. As a child, I was bewitched by nature. Our living room was

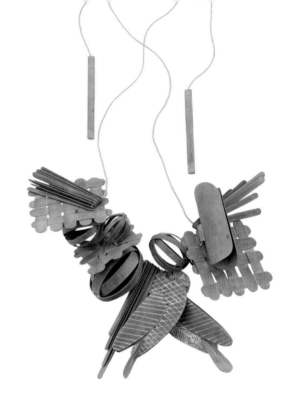

JARDINET
2007 | 11 x 13 x 3.8 cm
Zinc, antique fabric, rubber, rough diamond,
silver; constructed, soldered, set, glued
Photo by Eric Knoote

LOVEPOWER
2010 | 30 x 18 x 4 cm
Zinc, antique Venetian glass beads, nylon thread,
permanent ink; constructed, soldered
Photo by Eric Knoote

like a cabinet of curiosities because my father collected fossils, insects, and all sorts of strange antique objects. **WHAT DO YOU LOVE ABOUT THE MATERIALS YOU USE?** I love the language they speak, their character, their radiance, and the associations they invoke. **HOW HAVE YOUR SUBJECTS OR CONCEPTS EVOLVED?** My work has grown out of an inner necessity— I want to express ideas in my work, and I create the way I feel that I have to. I've developed through time and practice, through asking myself how I can increase the possibilities for expressing my thoughts. **WHAT INSPIRES YOU**

ORNAMENTAL GARDEN
2008 | 32 x 23 x 3 cm; 22 cm in diameter
Zinc, antique fabric, rubber, paint, nylon
thread; constructed, soldered, glued
Photo by Eric Knoote

JOIE DE VIVRE III
2008 | 10.5 x 9.5 x 5.5 cm
Zinc, paint, silver; constructed, soldered
Photo by Eric Knoote

THESE DAYS? Folk art. I love its honest beauty and intimacy. Folk art objects often have a mysterious radiance, because they're made with such care and concentration for some kind of ritual in a symbolic language. I'm fascinated by primitive objects that have a sense of ritual or magic purpose. Faith in the power of matter results in intriguing objects—jewelry made out of daily necessity, without any artistic intention. **CAN YOU ELABORATE ON WHY YOU USE ZINC IN YOUR WORK?** The color reminds me of the Dutch sky and the sea. To me, it represents the subconscious.

FLEURS DE STYLE V
2008 | 28 x 24 x 3 cm
Zinc, antique fabric, rubber, nylon
thread; constructed, soldered, glued
Photo by Eric Knoote

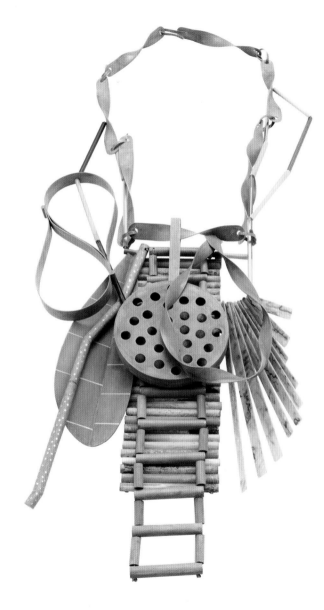

◀ A TOUCH OF MAGIC II
2011 | 40 x 20 x 5.5 cm
Zinc, bamboo, paint, permanent ink, glass,
nylon thread; constructed, soldered
Photos by Eric Knoote

"My work stems from an interest in the rich tradition of jewelry making."

T-V BRACELET 3

2007 | 7 x 10.8 x 10.8 cm

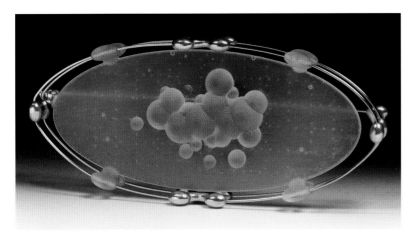

▲ **SATELLITE ARRAY BROOCH**

2007 | 5.1 x 12.7 x 1.3 cm
Sterling silver, stainless steel, SLA acrylic; printed from CAD
Photo by artist

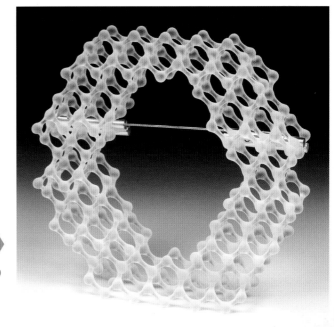

DIAMOND LATTICE BROOCH ▶

2007 | 8.9 x 8.9 x 2.5 cm
Acrylic, sterling silver, stainless steel; 3D
printed from CAD
Photo by artist

T–P BRACELET
2007 | 8.9 x 9.5 x 9.5 cm
Sterling silver, stainless steel
Photo by artist

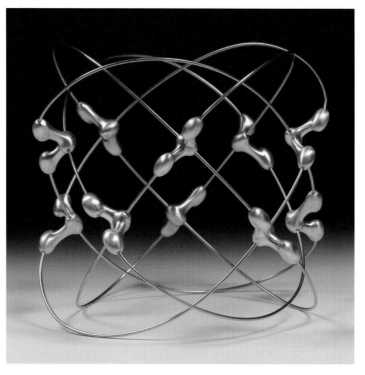

T–2 BRACELET
2007 | 7.6 x 8.9 x 8.9 cm
Sterling silver, stainless steel
Photo by artist

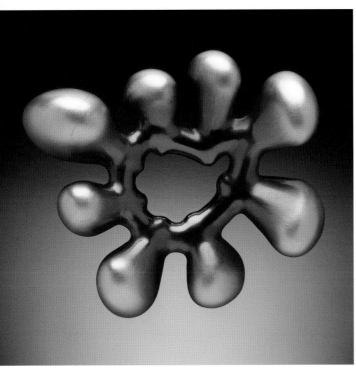

LOOPY
2002 | 6.4 x 7.6 x 2.5 cm
Silver, patina; CAD, electroformed
Photo by Dean Powell

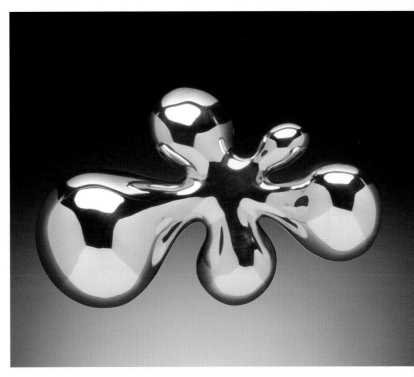

🔺 **SPLATTO**
2002 | 6.4 x 7.6 x 3.2 cm
Silver; CAD, electroformed
Photo by Dean Powell

Modeling a connector element in CAD. Cutting lengths of stainless-steel wire. Cleaning or preparing castings.
DO YOU THINK THAT COMPUTER-DRIVEN FABRICATION METHODS IN JEWELRY REPRESENT A MOVEMENT AWAY FROM CRAFT, OR DO YOU THINK THEY'RE PROPELLING JEWELERS IN A POSITIVE DIRECTION? CAD is a craft discipline that feeds into the creation of many kinds of work. It has already changed the way we make most things. If jewelry makers are inspired to take advantage of these methods, experiment with them, and find some meaningful practice, then, yes, the direction is positive.

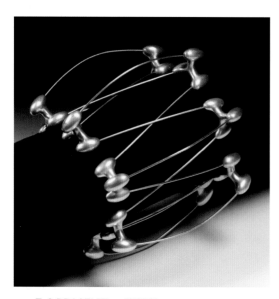

T–2 BRACELET—WORN
2007 | 7.6 x 8.9 x 8.9 cm
Sterling silver, stainless steel
Photo by artist

DOUBLE-SQUARE LINK NECKPIECE ▶
2007 | 66 cm in diameter
Sterling silver, stainless steel
Photo by artist

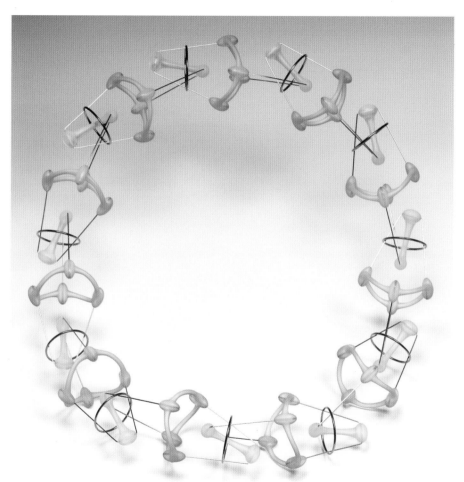

STEM-HOOP NECKPIECE
2007 | 32 cm in diameter
Acrylic, stainless steel, sterling silver,
patina; dyed, printed from CAD
Photo by artist

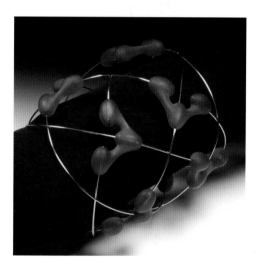

T-V BRACELET
2007 | 9.5 x 8.9 x 8.9 cm
Acrylic resin, stainless steel; dyed, printed from CAD
Photo by artist

SOFIA BJÖRKMAN
SWEDEN

"When I create,
I see things
from different
perspectives.
Making is a way
of understanding."

▲ **BLACKENED BRILLIANCE**
2011 | 20 x 30 x 5 cm
Wood, plastic, silver, string; 3D printed
Photo by artist

38

BLACKENED BRILLIANCE
2011 | 18 x 3 x 3 cm
Wood, plastic, silver, rubber; 3D printed
Photo by artist

BLACKENED BRILLIANCE ▶
2011 | 6 x 4 x 5 cm
Rubber, plastic, silver; 3D printed
Photo by artist

Q&A

WHAT DO YOU LOVE ABOUT THE MATERIALS YOU USE? I love the moment when a material tells me something I never thought it would, when a material surprises me and turns into something I never anticipated. **HOW DID YOU COME TO MAKE JEWELRY?** I was fascinated by a piece of jewelry about 20 years ago. It was a piece that affected me strongly. I then started viewing almost everything as jewelry. **HOW DO YOUR SUBJECTS OR CONCEPTS EVOLVE?** My subjects are usually prompted by philosophical questions. By making, reading, discussing, and thinking, I develop my work. I don't usually explore the same subject for long periods of time, but subjects can come up again and develop into something else. Time

 BLACKENED BRILLIANCE
2011 | 8 x 4.3 cm
Rubber, wood, silver, diamonds
Photo by artist

TIME ▶
2005 | 4 x 2 x 1 cm
Silver
Photo by artist

always matters. **WHAT RESPONSES DO YOU GET TO YOUR WORK?** Most of the responses in exhibitions and on the Internet have to do with the making process. When a piece is worn, it's the opposite; then the response has to do with what the piece is telling. **MANY OF YOUR PIECES INCLUDE FOUND OBJECTS. WHAT ROLE DO THEY PLAY IN YOUR WORK?** Sometimes I use found objects because of their inner meanings, but mostly I use them because of their patterns and what they tell

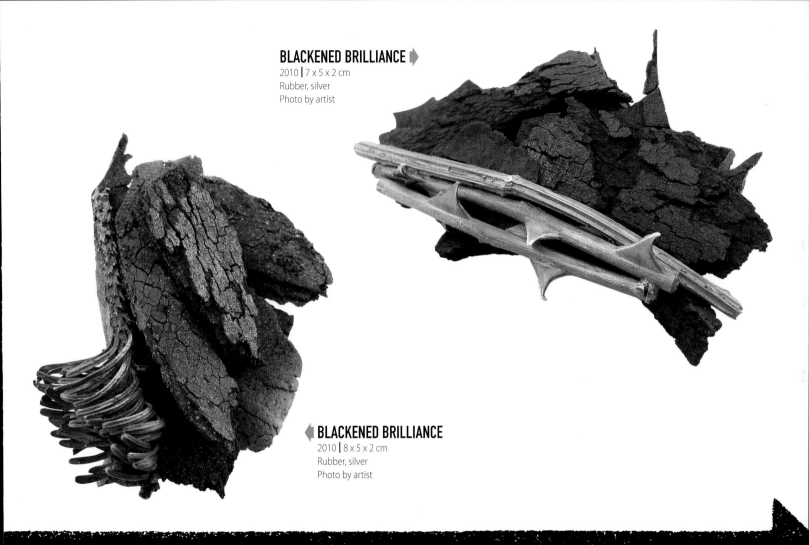

BLACKENED BRILLIANCE ➡
2010 | 7 x 5 x 2 cm
Rubber, silver
Photo by artist

◀ **BLACKENED BRILLIANCE**
2010 | 8 x 5 x 2 cm
Rubber, silver
Photo by artist

me visually. I think we notice materials and objects if they're put in environments that are different from where they normally belong. This interests me a lot, and it's an idea I often use in my work. A piece of junk can be exclusive in the right environment, and the opposite is valid, too.

"Through my
work, I question
traditional jewelry
conventions."

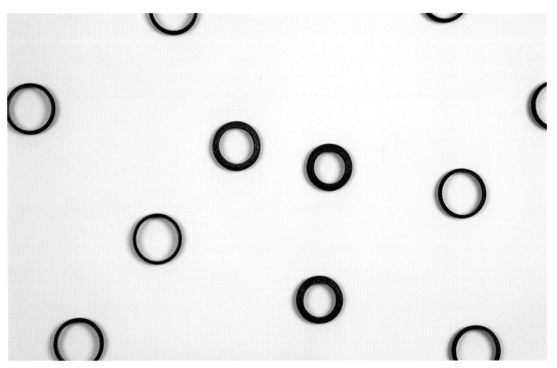

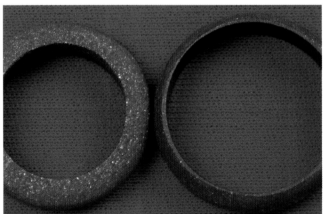

WEDDING RINGS
2008 | Largest: 1.8 cm in diameter
Magnet, lodestone
Photos by artist

A MASTER OF SELF-CONTROL NARRATED (SELF-PORTRAIT) BROOCH
2011 | 10 x 12 x 7 cm
Sleeping pills, aspirin, push-up pills, gold
Photo by artist

A MASTER OF SELF-CONTROL NARRATED (SELF-PORTRAIT) BROOCH
2011 | 10 x 12 x 7 cm
Viagra pills, gold
Photo by artist

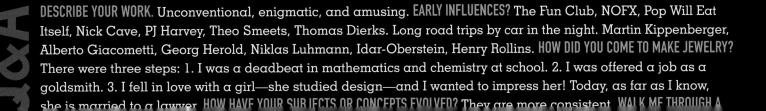

Q&A

DESCRIBE YOUR WORK. Unconventional, enigmatic, and amusing. **EARLY INFLUENCES?** The Fun Club, NOFX, Pop Will Eat Itself, Nick Cave, PJ Harvey, Theo Smeets, Thomas Dierks. Long road trips by car in the night. Martin Kippenberger, Alberto Giacometti, Georg Herold, Niklas Luhmann, Idar-Oberstein, Henry Rollins. **HOW DID YOU COME TO MAKE JEWELRY?** There were three steps: 1. I was a deadbeat in mathematics and chemistry at school. 2. I was offered a job as a goldsmith. 3. I fell in love with a girl—she studied design—and I wanted to impress her! Today, as far as I know, she is married to a lawyer. **HOW HAVE YOUR SUBJECTS OR CONCEPTS EVOLVED?** They are more consistent. **WALK ME THROUGH A**

DAY IN YOUR STUDIO. The music is always on. I have coffee in the morning. I usually do smithing early in the day. And I often consider throwing my iPhone into a river! As the day progresses, I'll do some filing. In the evening, it's red wine and beer. **HOW HAS YOUR TECHNIQUE DEVELOPED?** Sweat, tears, alcohol. Accordingly, I've had the usual war in my head about form. I never work on one project with one technique. I have two or three projects going at all times. But it's

DUOTONE BROOCHES
2008 | Each: 7 x 10 cm
Steel, silver, enamel, rubies, sapphires, black gemstones
Photo by artist

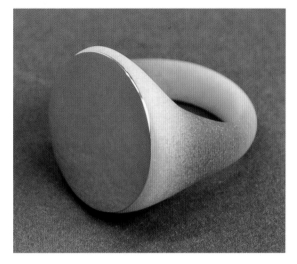

THE FISHERMAN'S RING (THE NEW POPE RING)
2010 | 1.8 cm in diameter
Breast milk from young mothers, gold
Photo by artist

DIMENSION CONTROL RINGS
2010 | Largest: 1.9 cm in diameter
Pure lead; set
Photo by artist

important to set the stuff aside. This can solve problems. WHAT INSPIRES YOU THESE DAYS? Fischli/Weiss, Gerhard Richter, Sigmar Polke, Willard Grant Conspiracy, Mogwai, cinema. Talking with Alexander Blank. Haruki Murakami and Truman Capote. WHAT RESPONSES DO YOU GET TO YOUR WORK? Double edged! CAN YOU ELABORATE ON THE PIECES YOU'VE MADE

🔺 **THE EGG**

2009 | Each pearl: 1.7 cm in diameter
Breast milk from young mothers, gold
Photo by artist

🔺 **PEARL CHAIN**

2010 | Each pearl: 0.7 cm in diameter
Breast milk from young mothers
Photo by Mirei Takeuchi

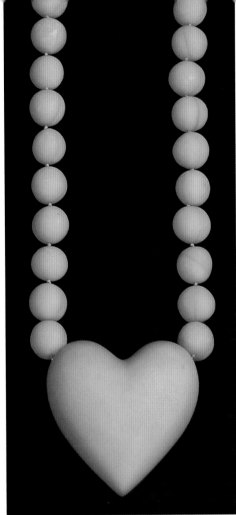

THE HEART (I, SATELLITE)

2009 | Each pearl: 1.7 cm in diameter
Breast milk from young mothers, gold
Photos by Katrin Demharter

LAURA DEAKIN

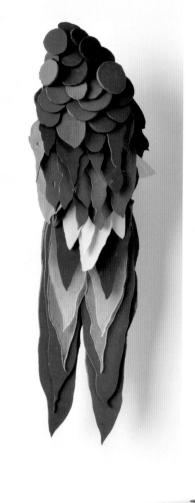

◀ **MOHO NOBILIS, 1934**
2010 | 12 x 5 x 3.5 cm
Polyester resin, pigment, plastic sheeting
Photos by Mirei Takeuchi and artist

◄ COUA DELALANDEI, 1834
2010 | 8 x 12 x 3.5 cm
Polyester resin, pigment
Photos by Mirei Takeuchi and artist

DESCRIBE YOUR WORK. Irony is a consistent concept in my work, which deals with a range of materials, from very traditional silver stone settings and classic pearl necklaces to unconventional materials like resins and plastics. **HOW HAS YOUR TECHNIQUE DEVELOPED?** I never did a jewelry apprenticeship, so my skills come mostly from my sculptural background. In recent years I've sought out traditional jewelry techniques such as stone setting and engraving. However, I love testing out new materials and their limits. Working with polyester resin has allowed me to learn about color, and this is proving to be a fun skill to develop. **WALK ME THROUGH A DAY IN YOUR STUDIO.** Jiggle the lock

CONFUSED PEARL EARRINGS (NECKLACE)
2008 | 61 cm long
Sterling-silver pearl earrings, freshwater pearls,
polyester resin, pigment; oxidized
Photo by artist

switch on the lights. Kettle on, apron on, tea. Decide on pigment colors. Choose shapes, and forms. Connect the exhaust system. Gloves on, mask on, mix part one, add pigment, mix part two, make and press the form. Wait. Repeat the process. Mask off, gloves off. Lunch. Mask on, gloves on, sand, saw, file, wash. Repeat process. Gloves off, mask off. Coffee. Clean, wash, dry. Read, draw. Switch off the lights. Jiggle the lock. **WHAT KIND OF RESPONSES DO YOU GET TO YOUR WORK?** One time a sweet old lady clutched at my arm, and pulling me down gently, said, "Excuse me, dear. Why don't you just leave the pearl necklaces the way they are?" **HOW IMPORTANT IS VALUE TO YOUR WORK?**

SPOONING PEARLS
2007 | Various lengths
Polyester resin, freshwater pearls,
pigment, synthetic pearl luster, thread
Photo by artist

HIDDEN PEARLS ▶
2007 | 67 cm long
Freshwater pearls, polyester resin,
pigment, thread
Photo by artist

Making jewelry from gold and diamonds has never interested me, because I never attained the skills to use those materials, and playing around with them requires money and bravery. Since I make jewelry from nonprecious materials, I don't worry about my work being stolen. Most thieves aren't interested in a fake pearl necklace or a plastic brooch. Having said that, from concept to realization, one piece can take a long time to complete. Add in the cost of a gallery, and the "value" of a piece can add up.

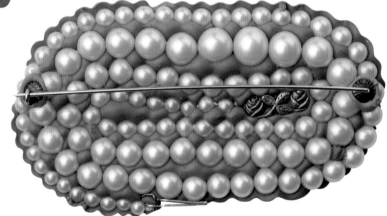

CONFUSED NECKLACE (BROOCH)

2009 | 5 x 7 x 2.5 cm

Synthetic pearl necklace, polyester resin, pigment
Photos by artist

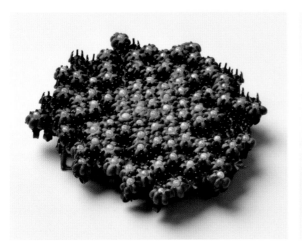

CONFUSED PEARL EARRINGS (BROOCH)
2009 | 8 x 8 x 3 cm
Sterling silver pearl earrings, freshwater pearls, polyester resin, pigment; oxidized
Photos by Mirei Takeuchi

CAROLINA GIMENO

SPAIN

"My work can be viewed as a manifestation of lines in space—lines that transmit life and movement."

FROM SERIES II: DRAW THE MIST—VARIOUS PENDANTS

2010 | Largest: 7.5 x 5 x 25 cm
Copper, enamel, silver; soldered, sifted
Photo by Oriol Miralles

FROM SERIES III: DRAW THE MIST—PENDANT

2010 | 8 x 6 x 4.3 cm
Copper, enamel, silver; soldered, sifted
Photo by Oriol Miralles

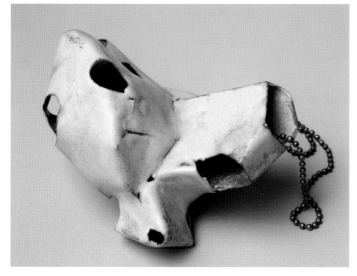

FROM SERIES III: DRAW THE MIST—PENDANT

2010 | 6.5 x 7 x 3 cm
Copper, enamel, silver; soldered, sifted
Photo by Oriol Miralles

Q&A

EARLY INFLUENCES? My early influences came from different fields of art. The work of Rebecca Horn, Esther Ferrer, and Marina Abramović interested me deeply. Sculpture, drawing, poetry, and photography have always strongly influenced me. The work of northern European jewelers, especially those from the Netherlands and Germany, influenced me to train in the area of jewelry and helped me better understand what is now my passion. **HOW HAS YOUR TECHNIQUE DEVELOPED?** I used vitreous enamel for several years while I trained as a jewelry maker. During the early years of my training, I developed pieces with flat shapes, but I've since branched out into creating new types of forms. Over the

FROM SERIES III: DRAW THE MIST—BROOCH ▶
2010 | 8.5 x 8 x 5 cm
Copper, enamel, silver; soldered, sifted
Photo by Oriol Miralles

years, I've explored the possibilities of creating three-dimensional objects by using jewelry techniques as though they were part of a sculpture process. **WHAT DO YOU LOVE ABOUT THE MATERIALS YOU USE?** I love the combination of metal and vitreous enamel. I love transforming the metal. Holding it, cutting it, welding it. Finding the gaps and the forms that can be created through intuition and observation. The enamel adds a contemporary element to these ancient techniques. I think that because it's a material that changes when heat is applied, enamel gives my metal structures an organic character. The constant magic of working with alchemical processes fascinates me.

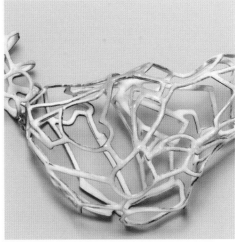

◀ **FROM SERIES III: DRAW THE MIST—NECKLACE**
2010 | 15 cm in diameter
Copper, enamel, silver; soldered, sifted
Photos by Oriol Miralles

WHAT INSPIRES YOU THESE DAYS? I'm interested in the idea of landscapes as places that live in our memories, that create links from nature to the body. I'm also interested in developing a language that allows me to combine several disciplines at once. **ARE YOUR PIECES WEARABLE SCULPTURES OR DECORATIVE ACCESSORIES?** My pieces are small wearable sculptures. The body is the place that supports them, the place where they have an identity as microsculptures. I always dream that the pieces I create can be changed in scale and become monumental sculptures.

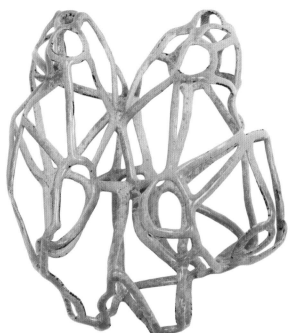

FROM SERIES I: PORTABLE OBJECTS—PHACELA CONGESTA BROOCH
2010 | 9 x 8.1 x 12 cm
Copper, enamel, silver; soldered, sifted
Photo by Oriol Miralles

FROM SERIES I: PORTABLE OBJECTS—BROOCH
2010 | 10 x 7.3 x 3.5 cm
Copper, enamel, silver; soldered, sifted
Photo by Oriol Miralles

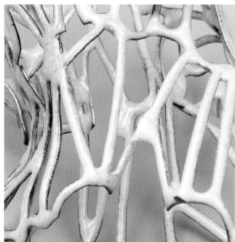

FROM SERIES III: DRAW THE MIST—BROOCH
2010 | 11 x 8.5 x 4.5 cm
Copper, enamel, silver; soldered, sifted
Photos by Oriol Miralles

'My work follows two different creative methods: a technical search for beauty and a conceptual investigation into Western culture."

AROUND THE WORLD NECKLACE

2010 | 64 cm long

U.S. dollar bills, Chinese yi jiao, South African rands, Australian dollars, euros, Argentine pesos, Bhutan ngultrum, British pounds, Canadian dollars; folded

Photo by artist

SIX NECKLACES FROM SIX CONTINENTS

2009 | Each: 70 cm long

U.S. dollar bills, euros, South African rands, Australian dollars, Argentine pesos, Chinese yi jiao; folded

Photo by artist

BHUTAN NECKLACE ▶

2009 | 70 cm long

Bhutan ngultrum; folded

Photo by artist

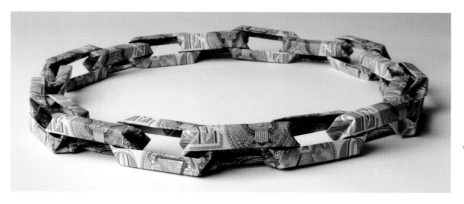

DOLLAR NECKLACE
2009 | 70 cm long
U.S. dollar bills; folded
Photo by artist

DOLLAR BRACELET
2009 | 8.5 x 8.5 x 4.5 cm
U.S. dollar bills; folded,
turned inside out
Photos by artist

SHOULDER CAPE ▶
2009 | 20 x 50 x 30 cm
Copper, polyester fabric;
electroformed, folded
Photo by artist

much later that I discovered my work fitted in with a relatively new folding discipline: tessellating origami. **WHAT DO YOU LOVE ABOUT THE MATERIALS YOU USE?** For the *Wearable Metal Origami* I love the interactivity, how I need all my senses to engage with the work. I love that I cannot explain in words how the material will behave and why and that there are so many other people (some of them scientists) who haven't been able to explain this either. For the money-jewelry collection, I love to work with the beautifully designed banknotes. Each note, with its colors, patterns, and drawings, gives away some information about the country of origin.

"I'm enamored with the idea of using the human body as a pedestal or a wall on which to hang a piece of jewelry."

◄ NECKLACE
2009 | 6 x 8 x 1.5 cm
Steel
Photo by Andrew Bui

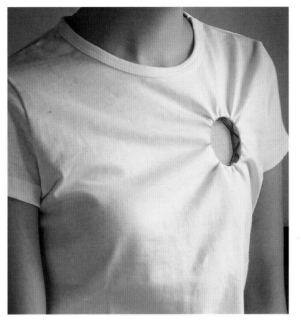

▲ UNTITLED
2009 | 7 x 5 x 1 cm
Sterling silver; constructed
Photo by Andrew Bui

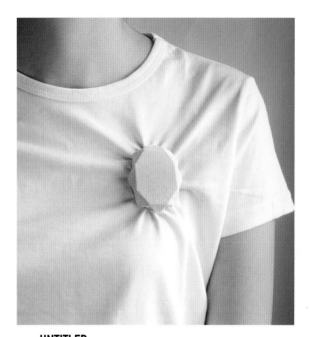

▲ UNTITLED
2009 | 7 x 5 x 1 cm
Sterling silver; constructed
Photo by Andrew Bui

DESCRIBE YOUR WORK. I don't want to categorize my jewelry as necklaces or brooches. I perceive my work as adornment for clothing. The pieces utilize the dialogue between clothing and jewelry and push the boundary of traditional methods of wearing jewelry. My jewelry is dependent on being worn. My pieces fully live when they're attached. **HOW HAS YOUR TECHNIQUE DEVELOPED?** I'm always searching for unconventional ways of wearing jewelry. Instead of using clasps or pin backs, I play with different ways of attaching a piece to clothing by wedging, pulling, or folding. **WHAT SUBJECTS OR CONCEPTS INFORM YOUR DESIGNS?** Function and wearability are indispensable elements of

UNTITLED
2009 | 7 x 5 x 1 cm
Sterling silver; wire constructed
Photo by Andrew Bui

UNTITLED
2009 | 7 x 5 x 3 cm
Sterling silver; wire constructed
Photo by Andrew Bui

jewelry since they are what differentiate it from small sculpture. Therefore, I want to make jewelry that functions as an adornment when it's worn instead of an adornment that could be attached. When one chooses a piece of jewelry, the relationship between clothing and jewelry is codependent. This relationship creates a boundary and limitation of size, weight, color, and more. I want to make jewelry that won't let the wearer use excuses such as "it doesn't match my dress," or "it's too heavy." I want to challenge wearers to see the "wrongness" as beauty. **WHAT RESPONSES DO YOU GET TO YOUR WORK?** Curious. Tricky. Humorous. Witty. People are either challenged to see my work as jewelry or

3D RENDERING EARRINGS
2008 | Each: 3.5 x 2.5 x 1 cm
Enamel, copper, sterling silver
Photo by Karen Philippi

HAIRCUT
2008 | 8 x 3.5 x 1.5 cm
Human hair, sterling silver;
hand fabricated
Photo by Karen Philippi

immediately get the urge to try it on. WHEN DO YOU FEEL THAT YOUR WORK IS FINISHED? WHEN IT LEAVES THE STUDIO? WHEN IT'S WORN? My work is very dependent on the relationship between the clothing and the pieces themselves. Therefore, the pieces are only completed when they're worn and there's a conversation happening between the wearer, the clothing, and the piece. I like the idea of the wearer always having the last and most important contribution to the

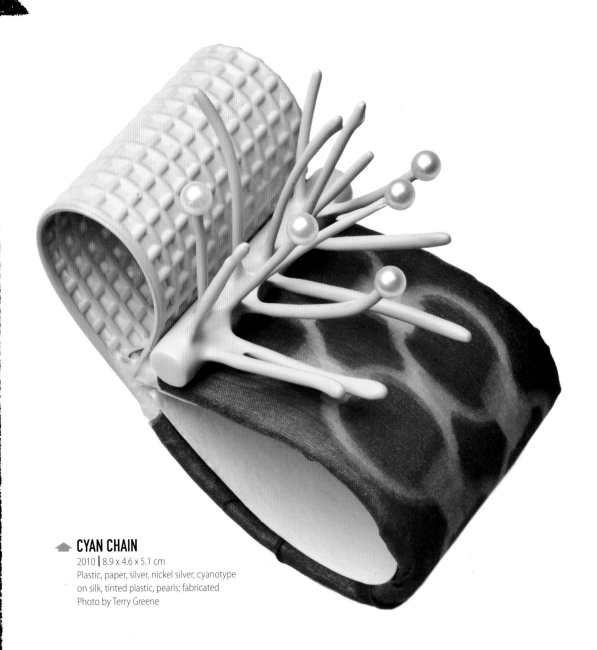

CYAN CHAIN

2010 | 8.9 x 4.6 x 5.1 cm
Plastic, paper, silver, nickel silver, cyanotype
on silk, tinted plastic, pearls; fabricated
Photo by Terry Greene

CYAN RING ▶

2011 | 4.6 x 3 x 0.5 cm
Wood, copper, sterling silver,
cyanotype on silk, tinted plastic;
oxidized, formed fabricated
Photo by Steven Brian Samuels

◀ **CONTINUED THREAD**

2010 | 12.7 x 5 x 1.3 cm
Wood, nickel silver, sterling silver, 22-karat
bimetal, copper, cyanotype on silk, tinted
plastic, cotton thread; soldered, fabricated
Photo by Steven Brian Samuels

DESCRIBE YOUR WORK. I create wearable, mixed-media sculptural forms with metals, wood, fiber, and found or up-cycled objects. My *Fluidity and Form* series features images transferred onto silk using the photographic cyanotype process. The mixed-media formations are covered in layers of tinted plastic. **HOW HAS YOUR TECHNIQUE DEVELOPED?** The techniques I use have evolved out of a need to go beyond what I've done in metals. I spent several years making felt, incorporating it with metal in order to create with more color and volume. I planned to felt through silk, but after I made my first cyanotype, it sat in my studio for a year. In the meantime, I experimented with many new

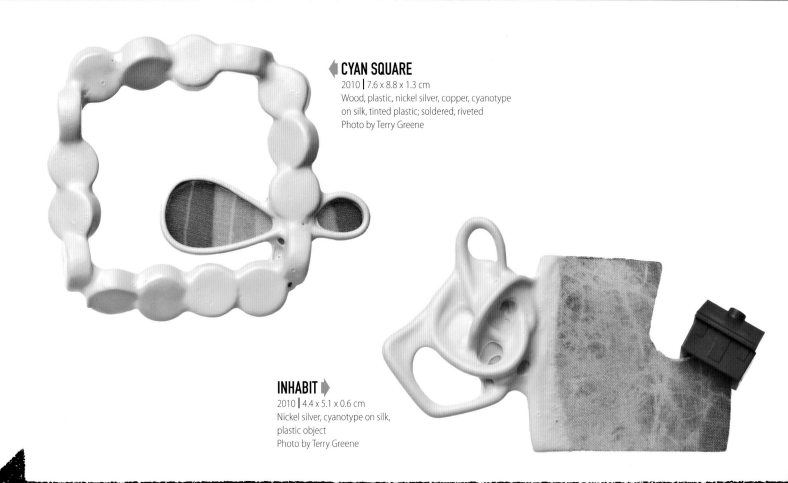

CYAN SQUARE
2010 | 7.6 x 8.8 x 1.3 cm
Wood, plastic, nickel silver, copper, cyanotype
on silk, tinted plastic; soldered, riveted
Photo by Terry Greene

INHABIT ▶
2010 | 4.4 x 5.1 x 0.6 cm
Nickel silver, cyanotype on silk,
plastic object
Photo by Terry Greene

materials, gaining the knowledge and control I needed to get the effects I wanted. I made jewelry with the cyanotype and plastic after trial and error, as well as after a number of what I consider transitional pieces. **WHAT DO YOU LOVE ABOUT THE MATERIALS YOU USE?** I really love their combination of controlled and uncontrolled qualities. In a way, working with mixed media allows for a looser fabrication process when compared to metals, and I enjoy the contrast. I especially like the way the plastic unifies and obscures the mixed media. It reminds me of the day after a snowstorm, when the demarcations of the landscape are hidden and mysterious. **WHAT INSPIRES YOU THESE DAYS?** I am

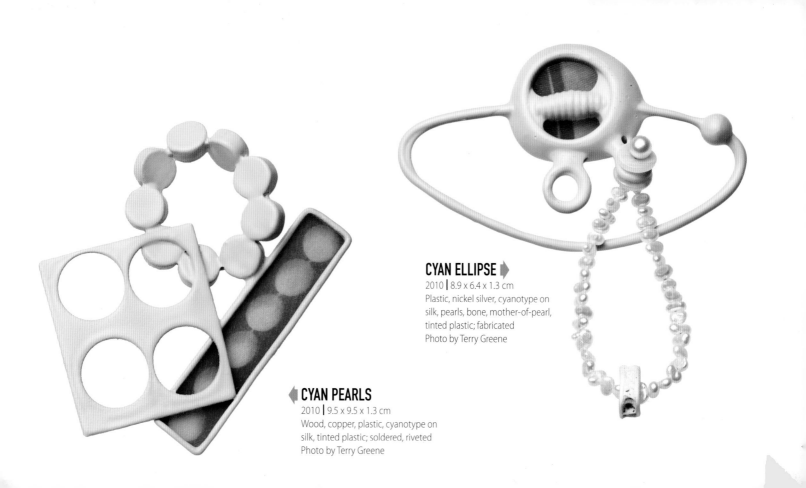

CYAN ELLIPSE ▶

2010 | 8.9 x 6.4 x 1.3 cm
Plastic, nickel silver, cyanotype on
silk, pearls, bone, mother-of-pearl,
tinted plastic; fabricated
Photo by Terry Greene

◀ CYAN PEARLS

2010 | 9.5 x 9.5 x 1.3 cm
Wood, copper, plastic, cyanotype on
silk, tinted plastic; soldered, riveted
Photo by Terry Greene

BEPPE KESSLER

NETHERLANDS

"

BONES

2002 | 80 cm long
Balsa wood, textile, Swarovski crystals
Photo by Thijs Quispel

ATTACHED ▶
2010 | 5 x 5 x 1 cm
Alabaster, brass, cotton
Photo by Thijs Quispel

◀ THE FAMILY
2010 | 25 cm in diameter
Gold, acrylic fiber, soapstone, coral, resin, alabaster, jet, bone
Photo by Thijs Quispel

DESCRIBE YOUR WORK. The focus is always on the materials and the combination of materials. Color plays an important role. My forms are partly cube-like, although never mathematically so, with angles and corners that are fluently round or curved, as if sculpted by the sea and the wind. "Little treasures"—that's how I describe my pieces. They're miniature sculptures composed of age-old and contemporary materials, brazenly combined and not bound to the traditions of jewelry making. **HOW HAS YOUR TECHNIQUE DEVELOPED?** I use a very limited range of techniques and tools: sawing, sewing, drilling, cutting, polishing, painting. I don't know how to smith, and I don't want

TIMELESS
2008 | 5.5 x 5.5 x 2 cm
Silver, soapstone, cedar, acrylic fiber
Photo by Thijs Quispel

ONE NIGHT ▶
2009 | 7 x 4.5 x 2 cm
Gold, brass, felt, wood,
balsa wood, textile
Photo by Thijs Quispel

to learn. Without smithing skills I feel free. I can follow my own route, work under my own conditions. I've always "invented" my own techniques. It's very important to me that the making process is visible in each piece; it plays an essential role in the experience of the piece. **WHAT DO YOU LOVE ABOUT THE MATERIALS YOU USE?** I work with all kinds of woods and with stone, bone, alabaster, coal, carbon, acrylic fiber, resin, and felt. I like that these materials

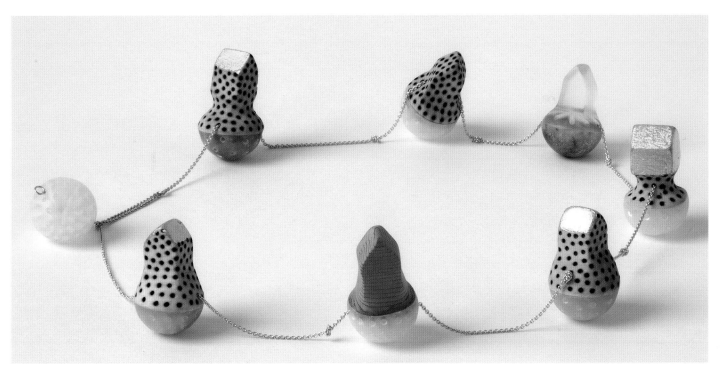

HOMESICK

2010 | 18 cm in diameter
Silver, gold, alabaster, balsa wood,
cedar, limewood, acrylic fiber
Photo by Thijs Quispel

don't have much form on their own. They have volume, which I can sculpt. I give them form. Any material that crosses my path must be explored for its possibilities, potential combinations, and limitations. **WHAT INSPIRES YOU THESE DAYS?** The material is always the starting point. I think via the materials in my hands. Other inspirations come from my heart and my head—thoughts about life and death, landscapes and seascapes, the movements

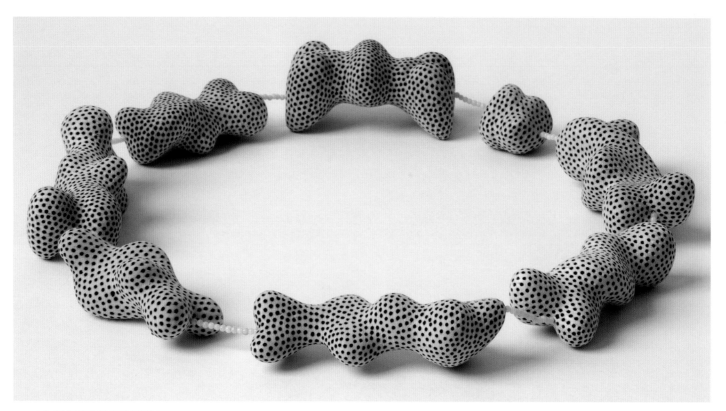

LA CONDITION HUMAINE
2011 | 24 cm in diameter
Balsa wood, coral
Photo by Thijs Quispel

of water and sand, the wind. Reduction is an interesting inspirational theme: How little do you need to tell something? And on the other hand: How many materials can you put together and still have the right balance? **WHAT RESPONSES DO YOU GET TO YOUR WORK?** The materials I use entice people to come closer, to touch the work, and ask

DESIRE
2009 | 7 x 4.5 x 2 cm
Silver, wood
Photo by Thijs Quispel

OVER AND OVER AGAIN
2008 | 5 x 8.5 x 2.5 cm
Brass, balsa wood, acrylic paint
Photo by Thijs Quispel

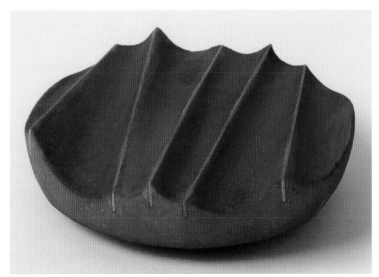

questions. My work surprises viewers: Some pieces look heavy and solid but are light as a feather. The questions about my techniques seem to be never-ending.

"I try to respond to existing forms and materials without using traditional goldsmithing techniques."

CONTAINER
2011 | 110 cm long
Zinc-coated steel, yarn; hand sawn, folded
Photo by artist

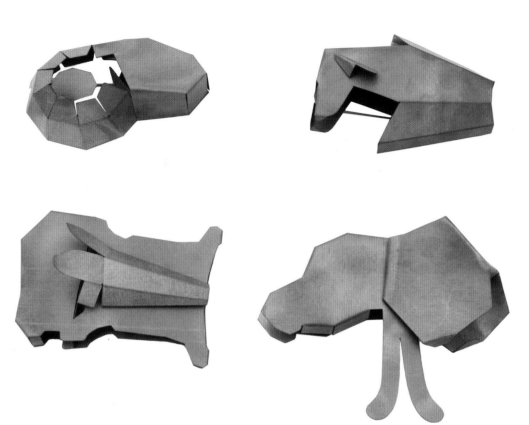

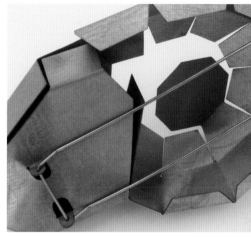

◀ **CHIMÄREN**
2011 | Various dimensions
Zinc-coated steel, spring steel wire
Photos by artist

DESCRIBE YOUR WORK. I reduce objects to the parts that I find interesting. The new forms that result are estranged from the initial objects or materials. **HOW HAVE YOUR TECHNIQUES AND WORK HABITS EVOLVED?** I am an early bird. While studying, I enjoyed going to the workshop in the morning before the other students arrived. This is now my way of starting the day and my most productive way of working. I use a lot of different materials. I am just as fond of working with heavy machinery as I am of doing persnickety things. While handling a material, I suss out the possibilities it has to offer. I try to work with the material in a way that makes sense. **WHAT INSPIRES YOU THESE DAYS?** I find interesting forms

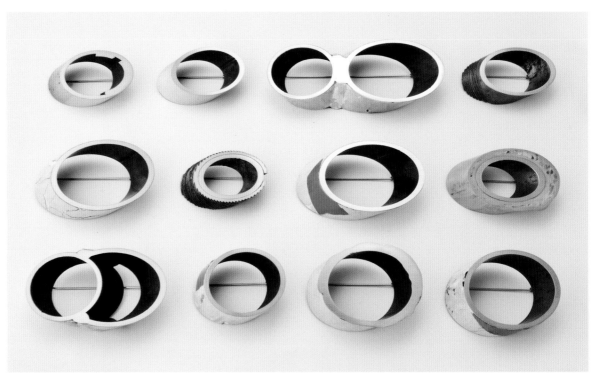

weißes KLAPPRAD
2011 | Various dimensions
Bike frame, spring steel wire
Photo by Thomas Spallek

in my environment—things and forms that don't necessarily look pretty but seem to have a special attraction. I take those things, analyze them, and use parts of them directly or interpret them into jewelry. **WHAT RESPONSES DO YOU GET TO YOUR WORK?** People are often curious about the materials I use. Some people wonder if the forms I work with already

◀ **SYBIL**
2010 | Each: 2.5 x 2 x 0.5 cm
Mass-produced costume jewelry
rings, heat-shrink tubing
Photo by artist

existed or were created by me. They're interested in the mixture of already-existing forms and elements made by me. **DO YOU BELIEVE THAT A MATERIAL HAS TO HAVE A RICH PERSONAL HISTORY BEFORE IT CAN HAVE VALUE IN JEWELRY?** Yes, I think that

HIDE AND SEEK

2011 | Each: 2 x 2 x 0.5 cm
Vintage signet rings, heat-shrink tubing
Photos by artist

CONTAINER ⬇

2011 | Various dimensions
Zinc-coated steel, spring steel wire;
hand sawn, folded
Photos by artist

"I'm a designer by trade, not a jeweler. My 'technique' is to design a piece, then figure out how it can be made based upon the design."

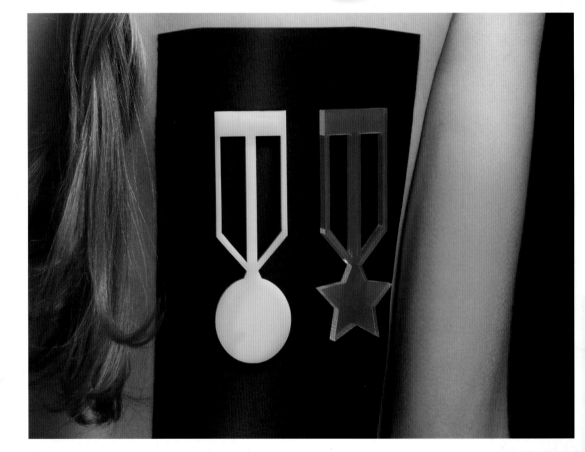

BUBBLE BRACELETS
2006 | Largest: 10.7 x 10.2 cm
Acrylic; laser cut
Photos by Lisa Klappe

◀ **MEDAL OF HONOR BROOCHES (STAR AND ROUND)**
2005 | Each: 9.5 x 3.3 x 0.5 cm
Acrylic; laser cut
Photos by Lisa Klappe

DESCRIBE YOUR WORK. At first sight, my work looks graphic and straightforward, mostly because it's often defined by archetypal and/or geometrical shapes. But there's more than meets the eye. Every design starts from a story. This story can be based on a material challenge or on other things. **HOW DID YOU COME TO MAKE JEWELRY?** I started in graduate school at the Rhode Island School of Design. My first jewelry class was short and very fast paced. I decided that for each project we did—and the projects were always based on learning a new skill—I would design a new piece. I very much enjoyed the fast pace—you have an idea, and you have the tools to make it directly.

▲ **VICTORIAN JOINTED JEWELS NECKLACE**
2011 | 42 cm long
Polyamide, finishing coat; selective-laser sintered
Photo by Lisa Klappe

Then you can decide if the design is saying what you want it to say, tweak it, or start over. After graduating I worked at a design consultancy, where I was encouraged to do my own projects. This is when I pursued more jewelry pieces. Later, I realized how much I enjoyed working on smaller, wearable items as well as furniture and tableware. **WHAT RESPONSES DO YOU GET TO YOUR WORK?** I receive many different kinds of responses. The *Diamond Ring* collection generates a different response from *Jointed Jewels*. The *Diamond Ring* pieces are something that most people understand directly, and a story can be created around them quickly. *Jointed Jewels* are different. Their shapes are

JOINTED JEWELS
2011 | Various dimensions
Polyamide, finishing coat; selective-laser sintered
Photos by Lisa Klappe

so simple that people either have a hard time seeing what's special about them or they can't stop playing with them. **YOU SEEM TO BE MORE OF A DESIGNER THAN A ONE-OF-A-KIND ART JEWELER. DO YOU THINK THIS GIVES YOU THE ABILITY TO AFFECT A WIDER AUDIENCE?** I do think it gives me a wider audience, but that's because I design not only jewelry but also tableware, table linen, furniture, etc. Jewelry-wise, the *Jointed Jewels* are my first one-of-a-kind pieces based on the type of manufacturing that's possible for me to do. I haven't pushed the one-of-a-kind pieces, but that's something that I'll work on in the future.

DIAMOND SILVER RINGS (LEFT TO RIGHT):
TOO THIN TO BE AN ENGAGEMENT RING, PERFECT DIAMOND RING SIZE,
A SQUARE, AND TOO WIDE TO BE AN ENGAGEMENT RING

2003 | Largest, 3 x 2.5 x 0.9 cm
Sterling silver, cast
Photo above by Mark Johnston
Photo at left by Lisa Klappe

**SMALL-TO-LARGE PEARL
JOINTED JEWEL NECKLACE**
2011 | 42 cm long
Polyamide, finishing coat, metal spray;
selective-laser sintered
Photo by Lisa Klappe

GASTÓN ROIS
SPAIN

"My work is
a metaphor
for what life
represents to
me: a game."

61°10'53"N

2009 | 8.7 x 6.3 x 1.4 cm
Marble; stonework
Photo by artist

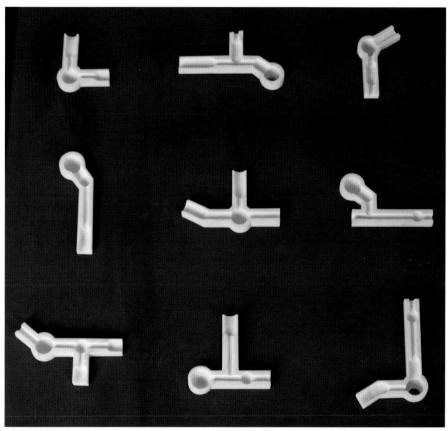

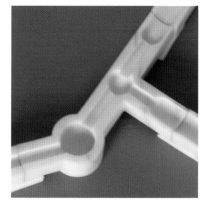

66°32'35"

2009 | 42 x 42 cm
Marble; stonework
Photos by artist

EARLY INFLUENCES? I've always been influenced by architecture—and by nature in its many forms. **HOW DID YOU COME TO MAKE JEWELRY?** During a trip through South America in 1998, I met an old friend who was an artisan and took my first steps in jewelry with him. But from the time I was a little kid, I felt a great excitement about anything made by hand or hand crafted. **WHAT DO YOU LOVE ABOUT THE MATERIALS YOU USE?** The dialogue I have with my materials is important. They challenge me, and I'm fascinated by the possibility of transmuting them. Stone was a new material for me, and because of that, I was attracted to it immediately. I wanted to discover it—that became my challenge.

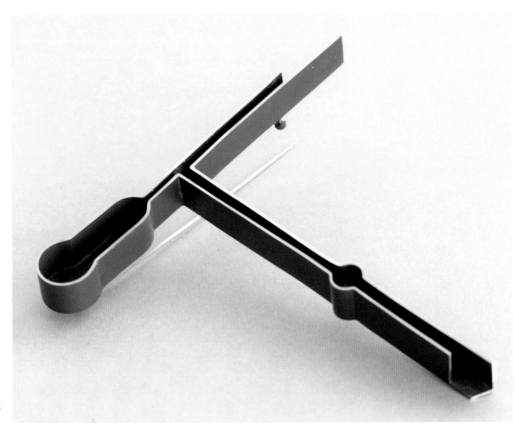

UNTITLED ▶
2010 | 9.7 x 9.9 x 0.9 cm
Silver; oxidized, metalwork
Photo by artist

The long working process and the patience stone requires have generated a more extensive dialogue than I've experienced with other materials. **HOW HAVE YOUR SUBJECTS OR CONCEPTS EVOLVED?** Themes begin and develop based on the continuous movements in my life—the constant searching, the making of decisions, the mistakes, the starting over. My internal creative process corresponds with the paths that I walk in my life. The movement turns into creative energy. **WALK ME THROUGH A DAY IN YOUR STUDIO.** A work day in Imatra, Finland: I wake up excited and restless with the desire to go back into the studio. I'm happy because I'm finding my way with marble, a powerful material. I bike to

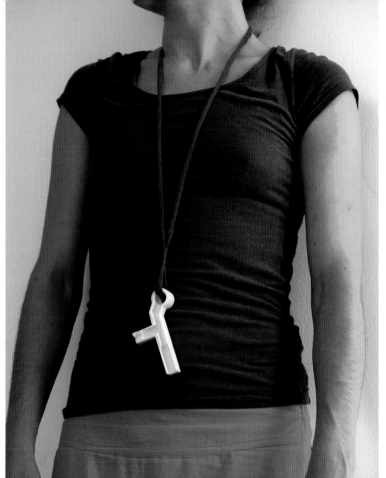

34°49'43"S
2009 | 9.9 x 5.6 x 1.4 cm
Marble; stonework
Photos by artist

the studio, and the road is a little bit rough. Everything is covered with snow! My beard freezes. However, I feel so alive. In the studio, everything is as I left it yesterday. I take my piece and sit in front of the carving machine. I press play on my CD player and submerge myself in my own world. I work on the piece with great patience and determination at the drill, making lines and trying to reach the desired depth. The work is extremely meticulous. I turn away for a moment to see snowflakes falling outside the window.

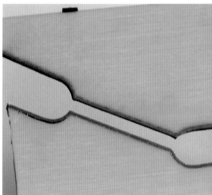

◀ UNTITLED
2010 | 5.6 x 9.8 x 0.5 cm
Polyurethane resin, nickel
silver, mixed media
Photos by artist

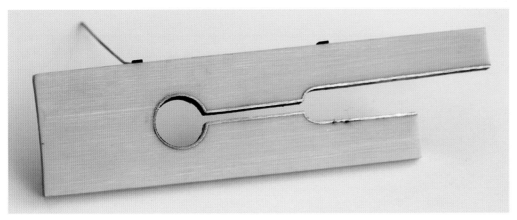

UNTITLED
2010 | 11.1 x 4 x 0.5 cm
Polyurethane resin, nickel
silver, mixed media
Photo by artist

UNTITLED
2010 | 12.2 x 3.2 x 0.5 cm
Polyurethane resin, nickel
silver, mixed media
Photo by artist

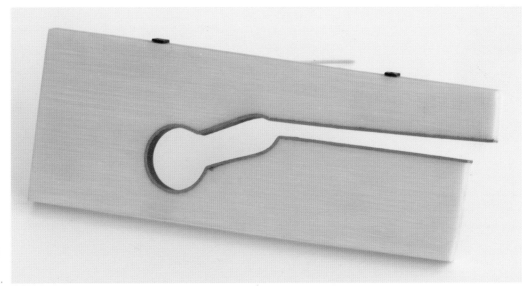

ÅGNES LARSSON

SWEDEN

"The idea of opposites is a constant in my work."

CARBO

2010 | 50 x 30 x 1.5 cm
Carbon, horsehair, iron
Photos by Carl Bengtsson

DESCRIBE YOUR WORK. I make necklaces from carbon and horsehair. My work is often rooted in abstract thoughts about the great forces that surround us, thoughts about life and death, growth and decomposition. With these words in mind, I've selected carbon—a basic material that exists in all living things, but that we also consider to be dead—as my main material. Some of my pieces have simple, basic shapes that refer to traditional necklaces and shields. The pieces look heavy, but they're rather light. Some of them are shaped on the body. **WHAT DO YOU LOVE ABOUT THE MATERIALS YOU USE?** I love carbon because it's a very basic material that keeps on surprising me. The element of

CARBO
2011 | 50 x 32 x 0.5 cm
Carbon, horsehair, wire
Photo by artist

CARBO
2010 | 45 x 32 x 0.5 cm
Carbon, wire
Photo by artist

surprise is a very important part of my creative process—and my main source of inspiration. Very often, I let my materials guide me. I think in collaboration with my hands, looking for expressions that match, respond to, and express ideas related to my themes. Often, I use opposites to emphasize different characteristics of the material that I think are important for the work. My other primary material, horsehair, is natural and has connections to life. **HOW HAS YOUR TECHNIQUE DEVELOPED?** I've never followed strict designer rules, and this has been liberating. I've always found inspiration in the materials I'm using and in myself. My work is a combination of the two. I've also experimented

▲ **CARBO**
2009 | 40 x 30 x 0.5 cm
Carbon, horsehair, wire
Photo by artist

▲ **CARBO**
2011 | 50 x 24 x 0.5 cm
Carbon, horsehair, wire, iron
Photo by artist

◀ CARBO
2010 | 35 x 14 x 15 cm
Carbon, horsehair
Photos by artist

◀ **CARBO**
2011 | 40 x 20 x 0.5 cm
Carbon, horsehair
Photos by artist

"I try to make pieces that act as a kind of art form and create curiosity on the human body."

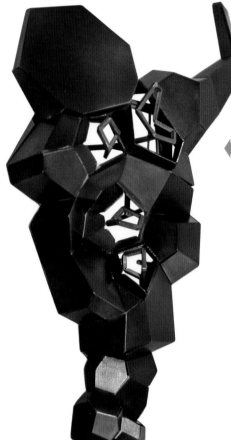

 UNTITLED BROOCH
2011 | 10 x 6.7 x 2 cm
Steel, oxidized silver; fabricated
Photo by artist

UNTITLED BRACELET ▶
2010 | 11 x 11 x 3.5 cm
Steel, silver; fabricated
Photo by artist

▲ **UNTITLED BRACELET**
2010 | 12 x 12.5 x 5 cm
Steel, silver; fabricated
Photo by artist

◀ **UNTITLED BROOCH**
2011 | 6.5 x 4 x 2 cm
Steel, silver; fabricated
Photo by artist

DESCRIBE YOUR WORK. I produce forms by using CAD and hand forming. I dissect surfaces to create visual pleasure from a variety of angles. When the light hits the surface of one of my pieces, it reveals greater depth of dimensionality. The final result has something of the look of abstract sculpture, or something between sculpture and the mineral world. **WHAT DO YOU LOVE ABOUT THE MATERIALS YOU USE?** I love the physicality of steel—it's cold and rigid. It's fascinating to turn this man-made material into something warm and beautiful. **HOW HAVE YOUR SUBJECTS OR CONCEPTS EVOLVED?** I create forms according to particular materials, formats, and functions, according to laws of structural

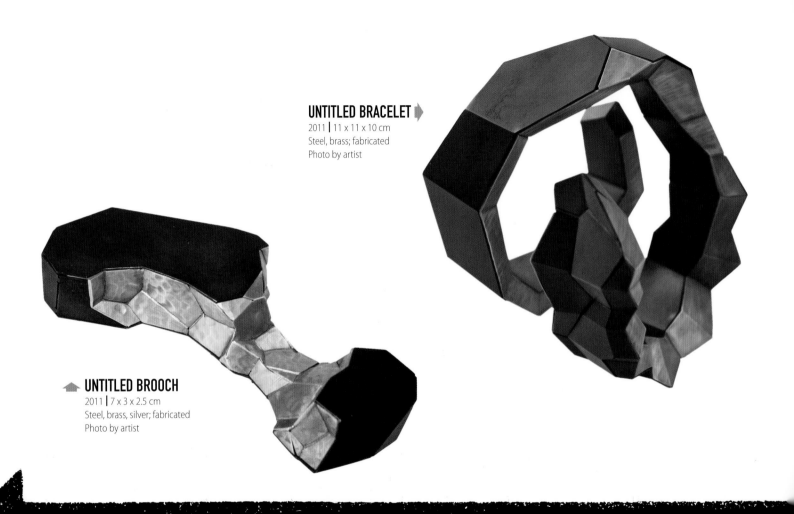

UNTITLED BRACELET ▶
2011 | 11 x 11 x 10 cm
Steel, brass; fabricated
Photo by artist

◀ **UNTITLED BROOCH**
2011 | 7 x 3 x 2.5 cm
Steel, brass, silver; fabricated
Photo by artist

economy. The basic surface of a steel sheet, joined to others, gives these structures their particular form. The nerve of a leaf, the geometrical elements of a mineral, a quartz crystal, or cubic pyrites—they are the natural structures of matter. I am subconsciously drawn to geometry and its mathematical arrangements. WHAT INSPIRES YOU THESE DAYS? Everything from dirt to high-rise buildings. I look around me and usually find new things. However, inspiration never comes when I try to capture it. Inspiration only emerges naturally, when I rejoice in life in general. WHAT RESPONSES

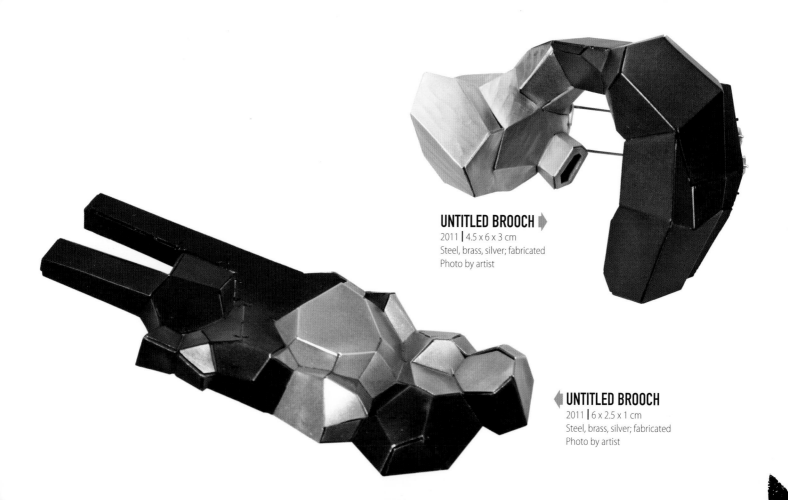

UNTITLED BROOCH ➡
2011 | 4.5 x 6 x 3 cm
Steel, brass, silver; fabricated
Photo by artist

◀ **UNTITLED BROOCH**
2011 | 6 x 2.5 x 1 cm
Steel, brass, silver; fabricated
Photo by artist

DO YOU GET TO YOUR WORK? Architectural, robotic, masculine, wondrous, origami-like, topographical, playful, seductive, elusive. **YOUR WORK IS VERY AMBIGUOUS IN THEME. DO YOU FEEL IT'S BASED SOLELY ON AESTHETICS, OR IS THERE A LARGER GOAL TO THE WORK? MAYBE A FEELING OR AN EMOTION?** Perhaps my work is no more than just the outcome of my obsession with making. I hope the wearer or viewer participates in my work by interpreting each piece in a unique way. My pieces are not mere renderings of content—they're expressions of things that cannot be said.

"With my work
I hope to create
symbols—objects of
personal revelation
or reflection."

◀ FEAR THE FIRST
2009 | 30.5 x 13 x 10.5 cm
Lambskin, river stone;
hand stitched
Photo by Mark Reamy

UTENSILS: WANT (COBBLER'S DAUGHTER) (UNSHOWN)

2011 | 72 x 15.5 x 5 cm
Pine, lambskin, silver, silk thread; carved
Photo by artist

UTENSILS: WANT (HERS) ▶

2011 | 61 x 92 cm
Poplar, leather, silver, latex, paper,
tulipwood, fox fur, silk, steel
Photo by artist

CAMEO: ANYA
2010 | 7 x 5 x 1.5 cm
Copper, found fur, wool, steel; die formed,
hand stitched
Photo by artist

CAMEO: CHARLIE
2010 | 6.5 x 5 x 1.5 cm
Found textile, copper, cotton,
steel; hand stitched, die formed
Photo by artist

leathers, the softest fur. Silver, silk, iron, cotton, wool. I shy away from plastics. I choose my materials for clearness of flow. If an object is clearly itself, if it can sing its own song, however faint, it's welcome. **WALK ME THROUGH A DAY IN YOUR STUDIO.** I like to have a few things going on at once, so if one thing doesn't feel like talking to me, another will. The most important spot in any studio of mine is "the wall," the spot where compositions are tested and important things are posted, posed, removed, replaced. Most days flow around the wall. The other work of the day is writing, getting digital, photographing, editing, posting. After coffee, I feel motivated to head out and start looking for stuff

FEAR THE SECOND

2009 | 17 x 13 x 10 cm
Deerskin, river stone; stretched, stitched
Photo by Edgar Mosa

UTENSILS: WANT (FIGUREHEAD)

2011 | 19 x 14 x 13 cm
Pine, found textile, latex, leather, steel, brass;
carved, hand stitched
Photo by artist

"I like working with materials and techniques that are a bit unpredictable, that have an uncontrollable element to which I can react."

FROZEN—NECKLACE

2007 | 55 x 55 x 5 cm
Polyolefin; thermoformed
Photo by Harold Strak

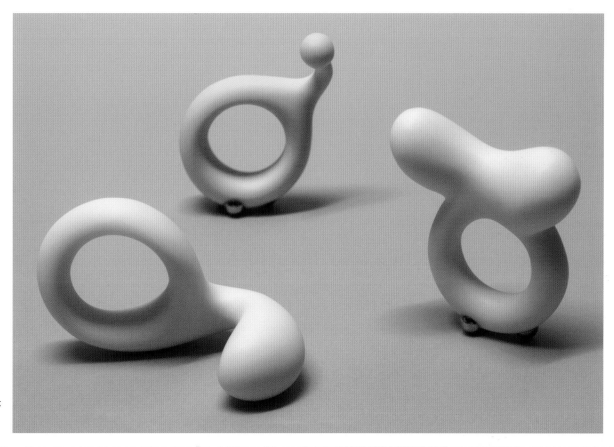

JOY ▶
2009 | Each: 2.5 x 2 x 2 cm
Epoxy, pigments, stainless steel;
cast, carved
Photo by Harold Strak

Q&A

DESCRIBE YOUR WORK. My jewelry lies in between fine art and design. Its platform is the body. I consider my jewelry completed when people wear it. Nevertheless, it's important to me that once my jewelry is taken off, it has an object value—it can be played with or looked at. **HOW HAVE YOUR SUBJECTS OR CONCEPTS EVOLVED?** In developing new concepts, I've learned to use my intuition more. My technical skills are broader, and I'm less afraid to push borders. **WALK ME THROUGH A DAY IN YOUR STUDIO.** My workshop is in an industrial area surrounded by harbors and hangars, and I get there by bike. There are different creative people working in the same hangar space. On this particular day, my

WRAPPED
2007 | 2.5 x 2 x 0.5 cm
Silver, polyolefin, wood; soldered, forced, thermoformed
Photo by Harold Strak

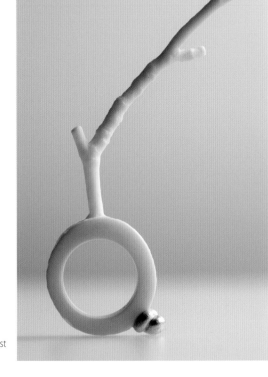

MUTATION ▶
2007 | 5 x 2 x 0.5 cm
Epoxy, pigment, silver clay; cast
Photo by Harold Strak

glass kiln containing a mold with loose glass frit is done with its firing cycle. I can't wait to see the result. I need the work to be ready this week, so there is absolutely no margin for mishap. The mold is easy to remove, and the green glass shines in the sunlight through the roof window. In another corner of my workshop, a small machine turns slow rotations to give the epoxy around a branch the chance to dry and harden. Some silicon molds with epoxy rings are waiting to be unpacked. My boyfriend drops by with sandwiches, and we lunch together. After he leaves, I build up

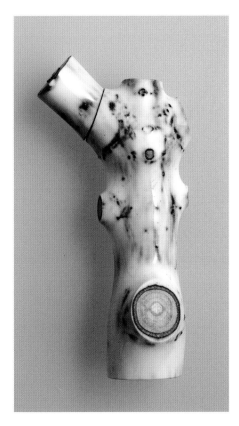

AMPUTATION—BROOCH
2007 | 5 x 1 x 1 cm
Wood, epoxy, pigment, silver; fabricated, cast
Photo by Harold Strak

ANNUAL
2007 | Each: 2 x 2 x 0.5 cm
Silver, wood, polyolefin;
soldered, thermoformed
Photo by Harold Strak

my wax models for another glass mold of plaster and ground silica. I need 22 glass rings for my installation. It'll be a fairly late night of repetitive rituals: casting wax, casting molds, casting glass. I love it! **WHAT RESPONSES DO YOU GET TO YOUR WORK?** A very personal, intimate relationship between the jewelry and the wearer develops as it becomes part of the personality of the wearer. I'm always surprised that different people with different backgrounds have personal bonds with my jewelry. It seems there is a certain universal language in my work.

▲ **GREENWOOD—RINGS**
2011 | Each: 1.8 x 2.8 x 2.8 cm
Glass; cast, polished
Photo by Harold Strak

GREENWOOD—BRACELET ▶
2011 | 10 x 9 x 4 cm
Epoxy, pigment; cast, polished
Photo by Harold Strak

BUNNY ▶
2009 | Dimensions vary
Thermoplastic; carved
Photo by Harold Strak

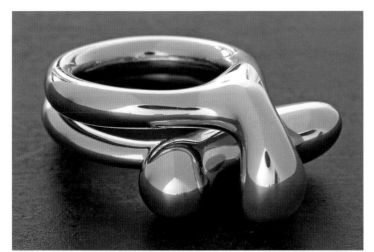

◀ **EMBRACE—PAIR OF RINGS**
2009 | Each: 2 x 2 x 0.3 cm
Stainless steel; cast
Photo by Harold Strak

NORA ROCHEL
GERMANY

"Flowers and plants are sources of never-ending inspiration for me."

◀ **PHYTOPHILIA**
2010 | 45 cm long
Sterling silver; cast, blackened
Photo by Janusch Tschech

WALLFLOWER ▶
2011 | 55 cm long
Sterling silver; cast
Photos by artist

Q&A

DESCRIBE YOUR WORK. My latest line of work is called *Phytophilia*, which means "love for plants." My pieces are modeled in wax and then cast in metal. Working with wax and exploring its specific potential is key to my fabrication process. The finished pieces, which are made from traditional materials like silver or gold, have a sense of seriousness and integrity that's contradicted by their playful forms. **HOW HAS YOUR TECHNIQUE DEVELOPED?** I work with a wide variety of waxes, from synthetic, plastic-like hard waxes to fragrant, high-quality beeswax. After working and experimenting with wax for some years, I can now model and cast large necklaces all at once, in one piece

UNTITLED

2010 | 5 x 4 x 4 cm
Sterling silver, rhodium plating,
emerald, ruby, zirconia; cast, set
Photo by Janusch Tschech

UNTITLED ➡

2010 | Various dimensions
Sterling silver, rhodium plating,
emerald, ruby, zirconia; cast, set
Photo by Janusch Tschech

UNTITLED ➡
2011 | 45 cm long
Sterling silver, porcelain; cast
Photo by Sebastian Lang

UNTITLED
2011 | 4.5 x 6 x 2 cm
Sterling silver, 18-karat white gold; cast
Photo by Sebastian Lang

UNTITLED ▶
2010 | 6 x 5 x 4 cm
Sterling silver, ruby, zirconia,
sapphire, peridot; cast, set
Photo by Janusch Tschech

EGG PUZZLE
2009 | 35 x 7 x 5 cm
Sterling silver; cast, blackened, whitened
Photo by Sebastian Lang

UNTITLED
2009 | 5 x 6 x 4 cm
Sterling silver; cast, blackened
Photo by Janusch Tschech

"Jewelry making isn't about inventing new things or working with the most innovative materials. It's about finding a personal form of expression."

MOUNTAIN BROOCH
2011 | 7 x 4.5 x 4.5 cm
Stainless steel, powder coat;
sawn, bent, folded
Photo by artist

COEPHENA BROOCH ▶
2010 | 15 x 8 x 3 cm
Stainless steel, powder coat;
sawn, bent, folded
Photo by artist

SEPHIMERA BROOCH ▶
2010 | 14 x 7 x 5 cm
Stainless steel, powder coat;
sawn, bent, folded
Photo by artist

▲ **LYSEA BROOCH**
2010 | 23 x 3 x 3 cm
Stainless steel; sawn, bent, folded
Photo by artist

Q&A

DESCRIBE YOUR WORK. My jewelry lies midway between the floral and the constructional, between living forms and manufactured ones. Some of the pieces seem like new species of plants or organisms, while others resemble architectural spaces and mysterious landscapes. Growing out of a single sheet of metal, each piece contrasts a rich, complex appearance with simple techniques and materials. I like this balance of extremes. **HOW HAS YOUR TECHNIQUE DEVELOPED?** I've always been fascinated by experimentation, which has led me to develop the essential guidelines for my work. I've come to realize that planning my creative process to the last detail stifles my passion

TASMALIA BROOCH
2010 | 12 x 9.5 x 5 cm
Stainless steel, powder coat;
sawn, bent, folded
Photo by artist

OVALIAS BROOCH
2010 | 11 x 9 x 4 cm
Stainless steel, powder coat;
sawn, forged, bent, folded
Photo by artist

while too much indetermination can also be an obstacle. Both my creative process and my technique have to live up to the underlying idea and the content of the final piece. Awareness of this led me to the low-tech methods I now work with. Sawing and folding are reductions to the essential and offer the directness that I need. **WHAT DO YOU LOVE ABOUT THE MATERIALS YOU USE?** Stainless steel, currently my favorite material, simply feels right. While being relatively lightweight, it provides enough stability even for the very delicate pieces. At the same time, it possesses an intrinsic stubbornness that provides a welcome challenge, compelling me to make clear decisions. **WALK ME THROUGH A DAY IN**

SYSPERA BROOCH ⬇
2011 | 14 x 13 x 5 cm
Stainless steel, powder coat;
sawn, forged, bent, folded
Photo by artist

⬆ **DROMALEAS BROOCH**
2010 | 13 x 8 x 5 cm
Stainless steel, powder coat;
sawn, bent, folded
Photo by artist

YOUR STUDIO. In the summertime, I open all the doors and windows or put my bench in the garden. In wintertime, I light the oven and make a mug of ginger tea. Then the adventure begins. I focus on the idea that has evolved in my mind, a thought of a three-dimensional form, a room that I can enter and explore. The form is very complex, built of different colors, structures, and scents. I capture the form, unfold it to the second dimension, and sketch it on a sheet of metal. Then the sawing starts, taking days, sometimes weeks. Every cut I make defines the piece more precisely but may also ruin it forever.

TIPINEA BROOCH ▶

2009 | 12 x 9 x 4 cm
Stainless steel, powder coat;
sawn, bent, folded
Photo by artist

◀ **DRUMONIA BROOCH**

2009 | 11 x 9 x 4 cm
Stainless steel, powder coat; sawn, bent, folded
Photo by artist

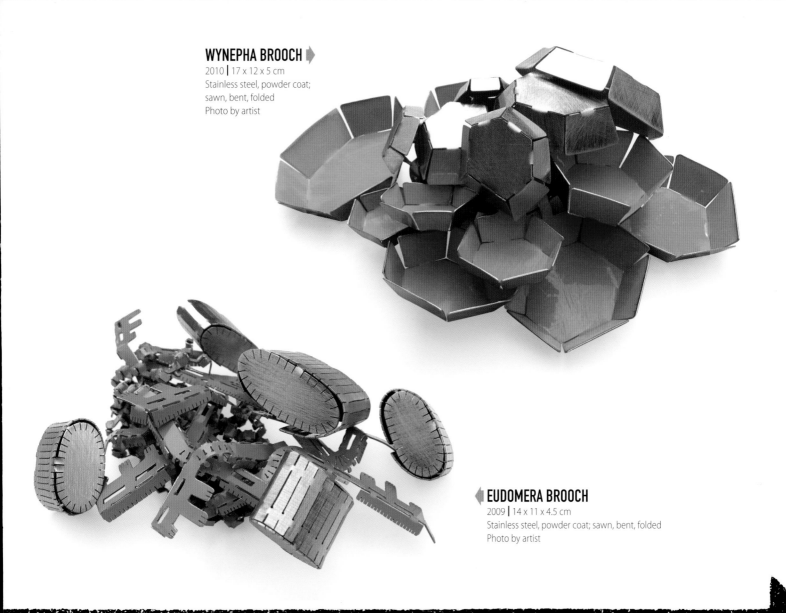

WYNEPHA BROOCH ▶
2010 | 17 x 12 x 5 cm
Stainless steel, powder coat;
sawn, bent, folded
Photo by artist

◀ **EUDOMERA BROOCH**
2009 | 14 x 11 x 4.5 cm
Stainless steel, powder coat; sawn, bent, folded
Photo by artist

ANDREA G. MILLER
UNITED STATES

"I make artwork to symbolize human functions within the modern world."

PERIPHERAL SYSTEMS, PART #4
2010 | 60 x 15 x 5 cm
Brass, copper, powder coat
Photo by Jim Escalante

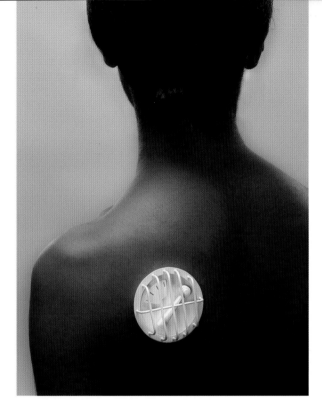

 **REGULATION, PART #1**
2010 | 8 x 8 x 2 cm
Brass, powder coat
Photo by Jim Escalante

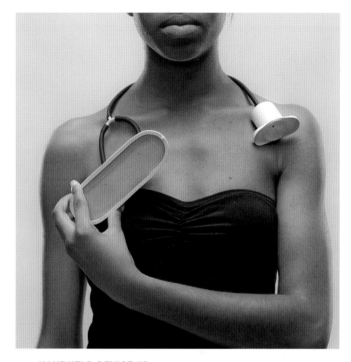

HANDHELD DEVICE #3
2011 | 18 x 40 x 5.5 cm
Brass, rubber, powder coat
Photo by Jim Escalante

Q&A

DESCRIBE YOUR WORK. My work reconstructs and interprets industrially made parts. My sculptures draw on the familiar characteristics of systems—ventilation systems, traffic guides, plumbing—that are meant to sustain our way of life. Some of the materials I use are ready-made; others I construct using traditional sheet metal and metalsmithing techniques. I alter common industrial parts in form, scale, and setting, then position them to interface with the body. **EARLY INFLUENCES?** Bauhaus art and design. The De Stijl movement. War and propaganda posters. I'm still interested in the philosophy surrounding these works of art—the idea that well-designed, functional images and objects can impact a society and evolve a culture.

PERIPHERAL SYSTEMS, PART #5
2010 | 60 x 15 x 5 cm
Brass, steel, powder coat
Photo by Jim Escalante

PERIPHERAL SYSTEMS, PART #2

2010 | 60 x 15 x 5 cm
Brass, copper, powder coat, rubber
Photo by Jim Escalante

PERIPHERAL SYSTEMS, PART #1

2010 | 60 x 15 x 5 cm
Brass, copper, steel, powder coat
Photo by Jim Escalante

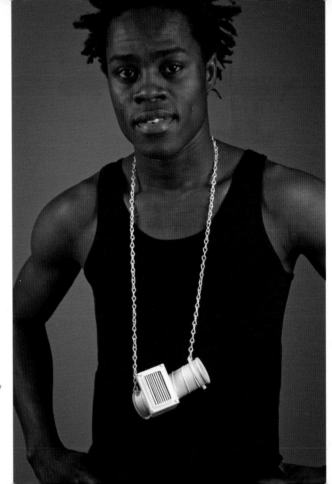

HANDHELD DEVICE #1
2010 | 5 x 11.5 x 5 cm
Brass, nickel, powder coat
Photos by Jim Escalante

REGULATION, PART #3
2010 | 15 x 36 x 18 cm
Copper, steel, powder coat
Photo by Jim Escalante

◀ AMIGOWIRTSCHAFT
2007 | 60 x 24 x 3 cm; 120 cm long
Fabric, string; stitched
Photo by artist

34

KINDER
2010 | 11 x 6 x 2.5 cm
Printed fabric, enamel,
etched copper; fabricated
Photo by artist

◀ FÜR D.
2011 | 12 x 8.5 x 3 cm
Printed fabric, photo made with a camera
obscura, etched copper, silver; riveted
Photo by Mirei Takeuchi

DESCRIBE YOUR WORK. Old family photos and recent photos are a significant part of my work. Everyone has a family, a story, and an album with photos from the past, but there are always new impressions and experiences in our lives that we can add to these. I've always been fascinated by old family photos—images of people very close to me and ancestors whom I only know from stories told in the family. **HOW HAS YOUR TECHNIQUE DEVELOPED?** Usually one element of a photo inspires me and becomes the starting point of a piece. By digitally working with photos, my goal is to alter the personal meaning of the image and to create a new vocabulary. Once the transferred image is on fabric or

SONNTAG
2010 | 11.5 x 8.5 x 3.5 cm
Printed fabric, etched copper,
enamel; fabricated
Photos by Mirei Takeuchi

metal, it becomes a new material that I can work with in an intuitive way. **WHAT DO YOU LOVE ABOUT THE MATERIALS YOU USE?**
The lightness and flexibility of fabric allow me to work spontaneously. If I'm working with metal, I tend to choose
a light one as well. **WALK ME THROUGH A DAY IN YOUR STUDIO.** Quite often I start on the computer, digitally working with
photos. When I'm sitting at my bench, I'm usually playing with different materials and photo-transferring methods,
trying to find the ideal one for the image. Once I find the best way to work with the images, I might sit for hours,

🔺 **GELBES AUTO**
2009 | 16.5 x 8.5 x 2 cm
Printed fabric, etched copper,
enamel, string; stitched
Photos by Mirei Takeuchi

days, or weeks just repeating the same element. This repetitiveness gives me the chance to think further about my work. **WHAT INSPIRES YOU THESE DAYS?** Saying goodbye to certain periods of my life through my work. **WHAT RESPONSES DO YOU GET TO YOUR WORK?** Because the images I use become so abstract in my work, viewers often can't recognize what it is they're seeing and are surprised once they realize what the images actually are—legs, for example, or little jumping men, things that aren't clear upon the first view. The lightness of the pieces is also unexpected.

◀ **BEINE**
2009 | 40 cm long
Printed fabric, nylon; stitched
Photo by Mirei Takeuchi

LAUTSPRECHER

2010 | 10.5 x 17 x 5.5 cm; 25 cm long
Etched aluminum, silver, nylon; riveted
Photo by Mirei Takeuchi

DORA

2008 | 9.3 x 10 x 4.8 cm
Printed fabric, aluminum, enamel,
string, nylon, silver; stitched
Photo by Mirei Takeuchi

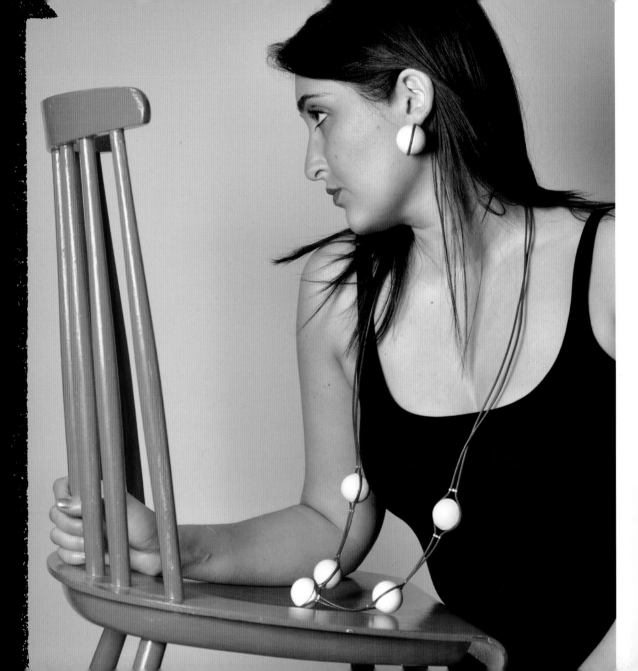

"Jewelry is the
ultimate art form
because of its close
relation to the body.
The body is a very
powerful tool of
expression."

◄ MOMENTS

2011 | Each pearl: 3 x 3 cm; necklace: 60 cm long
Leather, silver; sculpted
Photo by artist

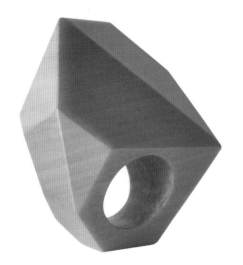

2010 | 6 x 4 x 1.5 cm
Wood, lacquer; woodwork
Photo by artist

◄ BLACK DIAMOND II (BRACELET)

2009 | 10 x 10 x 7 cm
Leather, titanium, silver; leatherwork, metalwork
Photo by artist

▲ BIRCH DIAMOND RING/SNOW

2010 | 5 x 3 x 1.5 cm
Wood, lacquer; woodwork
Photo by artist

Q&A

DESCRIBE YOUR WORK. My work is presented as jewelry—wearable objects and images that are sharp, a bit strange, and twisted. Often large and bold, each one has a background—a story to tell. **EARLY INFLUENCES?** I grew up spending a lot of time with my grandparents, knitting, embroidering, and crocheting. This was never considered craft in the modern sense of the word; it was a just a part of everyday life. I made wooden toys with my grandpa, and my grandma wove rugs. The making in itself was so natural to me that I didn't realize creativity could be used and performed on a professional level. **HOW HAS YOUR TECHNIQUE DEVELOPED?** My techniques develop through ideas

BLACK DIAMOND III (BROOCH) ➤

2009 | 20 x 15 x 6 cm
Leather, titanium, silver; leatherwork,
metalwork
Photos by artist

FASHIONISTA RINGS
2011 | Each: 3 x 3 x 1.5 cm
Synthetic fibers, lacquer; braided
Photos by artist

the "wrong" person. There are so many social limitations in jewelry; it's easy to play with the expected roles. This means that the wearer sometimes has to be pushed into something that's not comfortable, but pushing the boundary can create an awareness of your body and surroundings. It can make a special moment even more special if you're wearing something that makes you slow down or move more gracefully. Our everyday lives are usually so smooth that we can complicate them with what we choose to wear. It's like limiting yourself in order to remember how free you actually are.

◀ **FASHIONISTA BANGLES AND RING**
2011 | Largest: 13 x 13 x 5 cm
Synthetic fibers, lacquer; braided
Photos by artist

TIME MANAGEMENT II
2011 | 7 x 7 x 3 cm; 65 cm long
Leather, silver; sculpted
Photo by artist

"I format my
works as products
packaged for human
consumption,
inviting the viewer
to imagine a
relationship with
each piece."

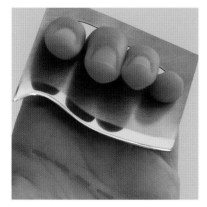

REDETERMINED DESTINY
2009 | 12 x 25 x 25 cm
Mild steel, brass, wood, paint, foam;
fabricated, etched
Photos by artist

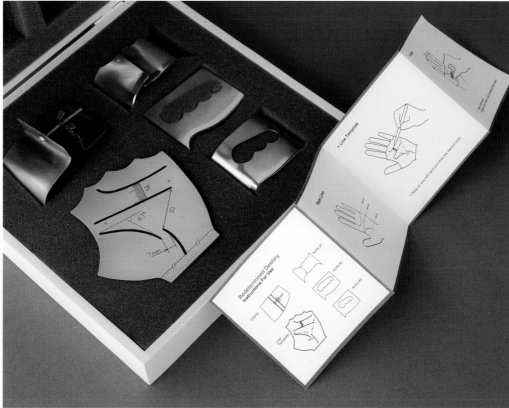

TERRIFYING BEAUTY #2
2008 | 20 x 15 x 15 cm
Brass, cubic zirconia; fabricated, set
Photo by Firat Akarsel

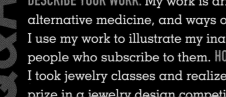

Q&A

DESCRIBE YOUR WORK. My work is driven by conventions and societal norms relating to the body. Plastic surgery, alternative medicine, and ways of predicting the future are belief systems with underpinnings I'm uncertain of. I use my work to illustrate my inability to reconcile the purposes, needs, and motives of these systems and the people who subscribe to them. **HOW DID YOU COME TO MAKE JEWELRY?** In the second year of my undergraduate education, I took jewelry classes and realized how much I enjoyed the making process. That same year, I got the second prize in a jewelry design competition held by the World Gold Council in Turkey and decided to pursue a career in

◀ **SEVEN–DAY REGIMEN: MONDAY**
2009 | 2 x 5 x 3 cm
Mild steel, raw garnet; fabricated
Photos by Samuel Sachs Morgan

jewelry design. **WHAT DO YOU LOVE ABOUT THE MATERIALS YOU USE?** I don't devote myself to a specific material. Between 2004 and 2006, I loved working with resins and plastics. I liked how fast they yielded results and enjoyed making color combinations with them. I also worked with drinking straws a lot around the same time. I learned how to use them, and it was fun to see the possibilities in such a material. Then I started working conceptually, and materials became tools to implement my ideas. I worked in brass, because it looked like gold in photos and it was cheap. I worked with steel when I was making tool-like pieces. I've also worked with wood and plaster. Honestly, I don't love wood

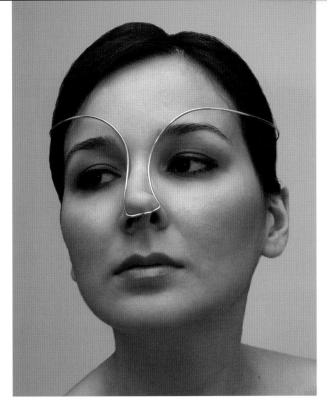

TERRIFYING BEAUTY #1
2008 | 20 x 15 x 15 cm
Brass; fabricated
Photo by Firat Akarsel

TERRIFYING BEAUTY #3
2008 | 15 x 18 x 16 cm
Brass; fabricated
Photo by Firat Akarsel

Metal is more familiar to me. I like the safety of working with a familiar material when I work conceptually. I've been working with fabric recently. It's quite a struggle. **DO YOU THINK IT'S IMPORTANT THAT JEWELRY HAS A MESSAGE, OR SHOULD IT FUNCTION ON ITS OWN?** I believe both are true, and my work consists of both approaches. I enjoy making pieces that have connections to the body, but I also like making jewelry that conveys a message about the issues I'm dealing with. Those pieces are often not wearable and are mostly pushing boundaries.

SEVEN–DAY REGIMEN: WEDNESDAY ▶

2009 | 1.5 x 3 x 3 cm
Mild steel, amethyst; fabricated
Photos by Samuel Sachs Morgan

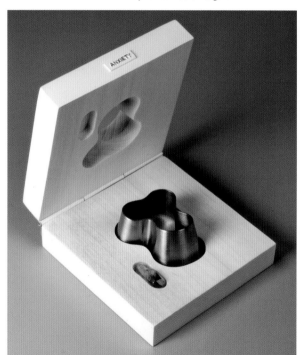

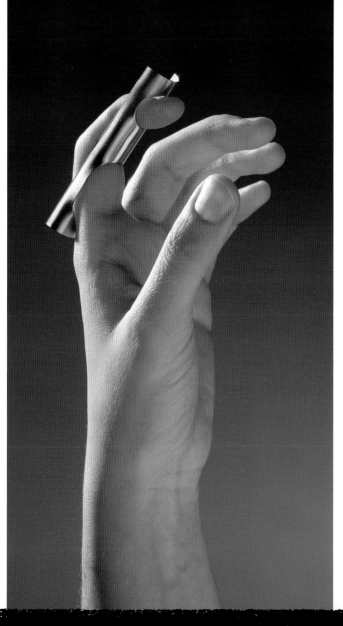

SEVEN-DAY REGIMEN: SATURDAY
2009 | 7 x 1 x 1.5 cm
Mild steel, green tourmaline; fabricated
Photos by Samuel Sachs Morgan

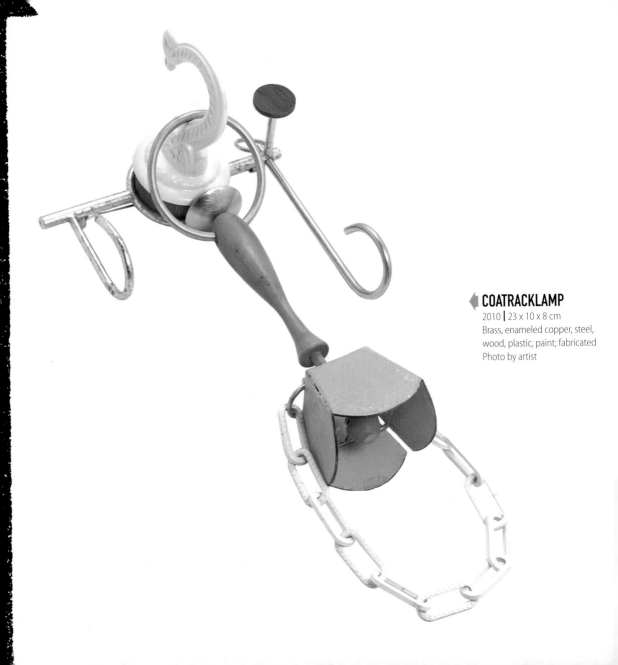

SETH PAPAC
UNITED STATES

"Jewelry acts as a personal signifier of taste, attitude, belief, and history."

◀ **COATRACKLAMP**
2010 | 23 x 10 x 8 cm
Brass, enameled copper, steel, wood, plastic, paint; fabricated
Photo by artist

LEOPARDANTLERS
2010 | 13 x 6 x 4 cm
Silver, brass, wood, resin, glass, leopard fur
from vintage coat, rubber; fabricated
Photo by artist

REDBLACKLEOPARD ▶
2010 | 46 x 35 x 8 cm
Silver, acrylic, plastic, polyester film, glass,
rubber, ebony, fur, resin, powder-coated
steel, silver; fabricated
Photo by artist

Q&A

DESCRIBE YOUR WORK. My work is an investigation and interpretation of the *parure*, an Old French term for a matched set of jewelry, which rose to popularity in early seventeenth-century Europe. The *parure* was modular and could be disassembled or remade to stay fashionable. An inherent narrative was created through this interchangeability. How does a collection of objects interact? How does this change when the collective group is disassembled? Jewelry for, about, or reflecting on a character provides the conceptual focus of the work. Through materials, processes, colors, and forms, my work describes settings or environments that in turn speak of a particular kind of character

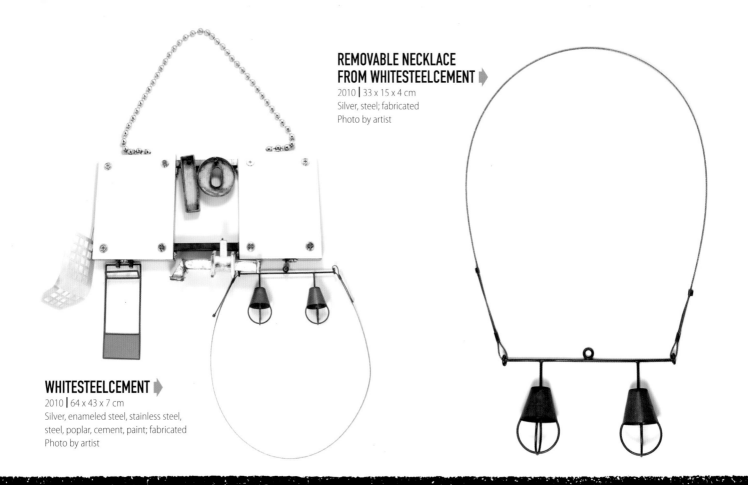

REMOVABLE NECKLACE FROM WHITESTEELCEMENT ▶
2010 | 33 x 15 x 4 cm
Silver, steel; fabricated
Photo by artist

WHITESTEELCEMENT ▶
2010 | 64 x 43 x 7 cm
Silver, enameled steel, stainless steel,
steel, poplar, cement, paint; fabricated
Photo by artist

or personality. **EARLY INFLUENCES?** The earliest influence in my work was architecture: approaching the body as a landscape. **HOW DID YOU COME TO WORK WITH JEWELRY?** I came to jewelry through an interest in architecture. Early on in my pre-architecture course work, I realized I hated the subject. The two-dimensionality of it was of no interest to me. I wanted to actually build things with my hands. That's when I was introduced to the work of Mary Lee Hu, whose masterfully crafted necklaces are architecture for the body. I realized I'd found a scale in which I could build with my hands using metal, a material that would allow for strict geometry, ordered structure, and an intimate context on the body. **HOW DO YOUR SUBJECTS OR CONCEPTS EVOLVE?** My work is always sequential. One body of work follows from

◄ ORANGESHAGFAUXWOOD
2010 | 61 x 38 x 15 cm
Silver, brass, copper, steel, enamel, wood, plastic,
rubber, wool, paint, gold; fabricated, knitted
Photos by artist

HYPHAE | RIVER AND RIVULET BANGLES

2011 | Each: 8.9 x 11.8 x 2 cm
Nylon, acrylic lacquer; 3D printed by selective-laser
sintering, coated
Photo by artists

HYPHAE | HYPHAE RINGS

2011 | Each: 3.3 x 3.3 x 3.3 cm
Stainless steel, bronze infused;
3D printed
Photo by artists

HYPHAE | VESSEL PENDANT

2011 | 4.7 x 6.2 x 1.2 cm
Sterling silver; lost wax casting
from 3D-printed wax
Photo by artists

Q&A

DESCRIBE YOUR WORK. We work with computation and digital fabrication to create not just single objects, but processes that can generate an infinite variety of forms. Our designs are based on natural phenomena, which we approximate and adapt by creating computer simulations that mimic these phenomena. We add constraints and interactivity to sculpt these systems to our specific design goals. **EARLY INFLUENCES?** Jesse's interest in math and computer science was inspired by early researchers of complex systems and artificial intelligence. Jessica's interest in microscopic structures formed after observing protozoa and algae under a microscope. While studying biology at the Massachusetts Institute

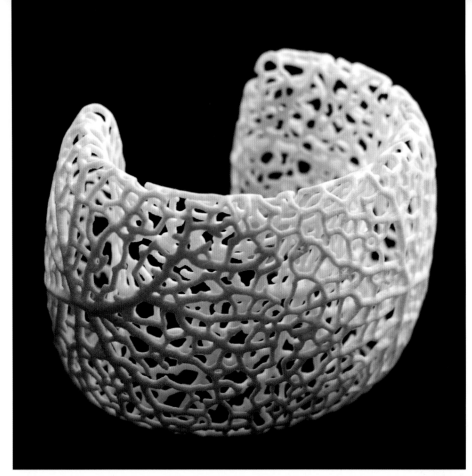

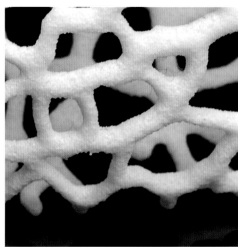

HYPHAE | RHIZOME CUFF
2011 | 6.3 x 8.3 x 5.1 cm
Nylon, acrylic lacquer; 3D printed by
selective-laser sintering, coated
Photos by artists

of Technology, she became fascinated with the complex mechanisms behind the behavior and morphology of living things. **HOW HAS YOUR TECHNIQUE DEVELOPED?** When we first started, we created simple simulations in 2D. We now use more sophisticated simulation and computational geometry methods to create intricate 3D forms. We've become masters of 3D printing. **WHAT DO YOU LOVE ABOUT THE MATERIALS YOU USE?** Our primary material is code. We don't actually work with the physical processes that manifest our work. There are a lot of great things about working with code. Anything that you do can be directly reused and built upon in the future through copy-and-paste. The tedious parts of design are done

◀ **DENDRITE | FULL MOON NECKLACE SERIES**

2007 | Pendant: 5 x 5 x 0.1 cm
Stainless steel; photochemically etched
Photo by Sarah Renard

automatically. This means we can iterate hundreds of possibilities in a short period of time. **A LOT OF YOUR WORK IS BASED ON INPUT FROM USERS. DO YOU BELIEVE THAT THIS IS A FORM OF DEMOCRATIC DESIGN?** Not exactly. It's part of an effort to democratize our design process, not so much in the sense of a user injecting his own intentionality into the product. The apps we create are simplified versions of the systems we use, and their purpose is to engage people in our process. We also make the source code available, so people see what we're doing to create the forms. We think that opening up our

▲ **CELL CYCLE | TWO-LAYER TWIST RING**
2009 | 2.6 x 2.6 x 1.7 cm
Sterling silver; lost wax cast from 3D-printed wax
Photo by artists

◀ **CELL CYCLE | MORPH BANGLE**
2010 | 7.9 x 7.9 x 2.6 cm
Bronze-infused stainless steel; 3D printed
Photo by artists

HYPHAE | HYPHAE BROOCH ⬇

2011 | 7.7 x 7.7 x 2.4 cm
Nylon, acrylic lacquer; 3D printed by
selective-laser sintering, coated
Photo by artists

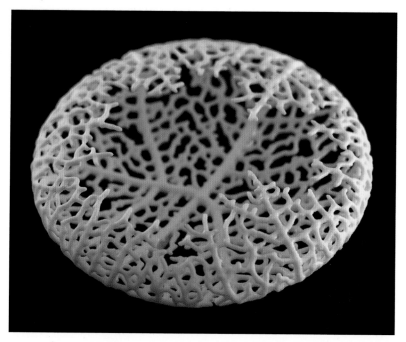

🔺 CELL CYCLE | WAVE BRACELET

2009 | 8.3 x 8.2 x 5.1 cm
Nylon, acrylic lacquer; 3D printed by
selective-laser sintering, dyed, coated
Photo by artists

"I want to make pieces that contain a measure of qualitative and aesthetic tension. I like taking risks with my work."

FROM THE APARTFROM COLLECTION

2005 | 25 cm in diameter
Gold-plated chain, electrical cord, gold-plated brass
Photo by Michael Grenmarker

FROM THE APARTFROM COLLECTION ▶

2005 | 25 cm in diameter
Gold-plated chain, rubber-dipped sock,
gold-plated brass
Photos by Michael Grenmarker

Q&A

EARLY INFLUENCES? Louise Bourgeois, because of her breadth. She wasn't bound by specific materials and traditions. Elsa Schiaparelli, because she pioneered a surrealistic way of thinking and working. Her combination of fashion and art still impresses me. **HOW HAS YOUR TECHNIQUE DEVELOPED?** In the beginning I worked with traditional silversmithing techniques. When I mastered them, I felt a freedom and a need to expand my skills. After spending a few years polishing silver and gold, giving them a "perfect" finish, I'd had enough. I needed to do something completely different—to pursue the opposite of a "perfect" finish. This led me to work with everything from plywood

FROM THE TAKE YOUR SEAT COLLECTION
2001 | 10 x 15 x 7 cm
Leather, horsehair, rivets, plywood
Photo by Anna-Mia Brolund

FROM THE TAKE YOUR SEAT COLLECTION ➡
2001 | 42 x 35 x 10 cm
Leather, horsehair, rivets, plywood
Photo by Anna-Mia Brolund

and wooden sticks to rubber and used clothes. I think my knowledge and understanding of metal have allowed me to approach these materials from new and unexpected angles. WALK ME THROUGH A DAY IN YOUR STUDIO. If I'm starting a new project, I'll spend time collecting images that in some way appeal to me. I take a lot of photos and work with them on my computer. I also spend time on the Internet searching for images that speak to me. I often don't really know what I'm looking for, but after a while a certain mood takes shape in my research. Then I collect materials and start making the jewelry. I work fast and have to force myself to stop before the pieces get overworked. HOW HAVE YOUR SUBJECTS OR CONCEPTS EVOLVED? I used to focus on specific topics and themes, and my jewelry functioned as a kind of

FROM THE IN THE ACT COLLECTION ➧

2007 | 28 cm in diameter
Silver, plywood, foam, latex, graphite
Photo by artist

◀ **FROM THE TAKE YOUR SEAT COLLECTION**

2001 | 30 x 35 x 10 cm
Leather, horsehair, rivets, plywood
Photo by Anna-Mia Brolund

commentary or solution to a social problem, or whatever the theme was. But lately my jewelry has been less about topics and issues and more about shape, color, and proportion and the vibrating tension between these elements. At the end of the day, each piece has to be able to stand by itself without being explained. **TALK A BIT ABOUT THE MATERIALS YOU USE.** I really like materials that aren't traditional. Plywood and rubber don't have the inherent value of materials traditionally used by jewelers. When I'm making jewelry, I put myself in a state of mind where I pretend. I give the material "new" value. I treat it as if it has real significance, as if it is really important without being exclusive and expensive.

PIA ALEBORG 165

"Jewelry is
decoration for
the body, but that
doesn't mean
it can't have
significance or
a message."

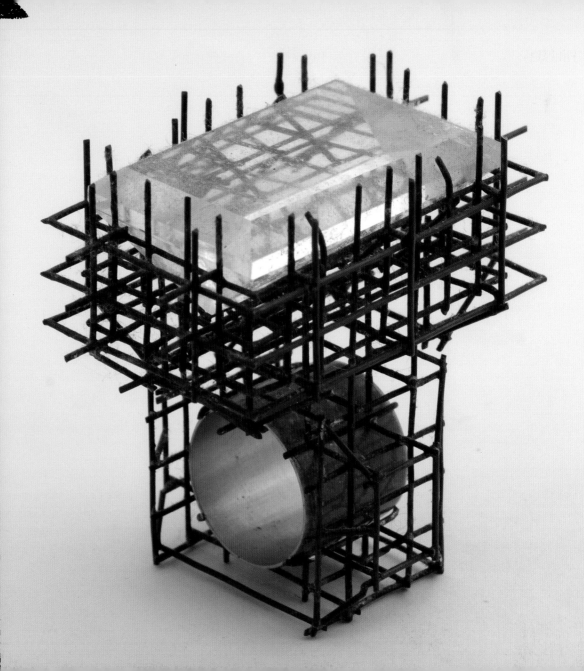

PINK RING

2009 | 6 x 3 x 4 cm
Silver, gold, enamel, rock crystal; fabricated, set
Photo by artist

UNTITLED

2009 | 2 x 2 cm
Gold, black diamond; fabricated, set
Photos by artist

DESCRIBE YOUR WORK. I make wearable jewelry using materials such as gold, silver, and semiprecious stones. I create clear, geometrical designs. They look like well-reasoned works, but in reality they're based on irrational, instinctual choices. Lately, I've been adding elements of graffiti. My work is about repetition. I love making pieces that have a sense of rhythm, that change perspectives. **HOW HAS YOUR TECHNIQUE DEVELOPED?** At one point in time, I wanted to be the best technical goldsmith in the world, so I tried to work for companies where I could learn the trade. Nowadays, I don't care so much about that. I just want to express myself. **EARLY INFLUENCES?** Architecture and

UNTITLED
2008 | 2 x 2 x 1.5 cm
Gold, brown diamonds; fabricated, set
Photo by artist

UNTITLED
2007 | 2 x 2 x 1.5 cm
Gold, aquamarine; fabricated, set
Photo by artist

rhythm. **HOW HAVE YOUR SUBJECTS OR CONCEPTS EVOLVED?** In the beginning, I wanted to make nice technical pieces. Now I want to tell stories. Aesthetics are still important to me, but I don't want to show off my technique. Titles are becoming more and more important to me. **WALK ME THROUGH A DAY IN YOUR STUDIO.** When I want to make a piece, I just work. Drink coffee and work again—but only if the place is in complete order. When my studio is

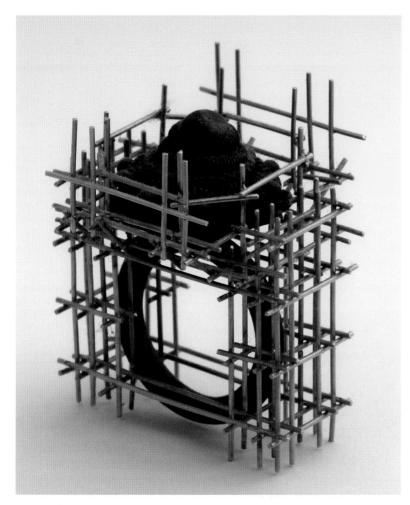

▲ **FOR EVER**
2010 | 2 x 2 x 1.5 cm
Wood; cut, carved
Photo by artist

◄ **RING UNDER CONSTRUCTION**
2006 | 5 x 4 x 2.5 cm
Gold, silver; fabricated
Photo by artist

a mess I get distracted. Then I go to my DJ turntable or call friends. DO YOU FEEL THAT THE MINI SCAFFOLDING IN YOUR WORK IS FOR THE WEARER OR FOR OTHER ARTISTS? I do make it for the wearer, but I'm now realizing that probably only

HISTORY REPEATS ▶

2010 | 5 x 3 x 4 cm
Silver, part of the Berlin wall,
spray paint; fabricated
Photos by artist

PAINT JOB, RED

2011 | Each: 4 x 2 x 1.5 cm
Silver, rock crystal, spray paint;
fabricated, set
Photo by artist

NECESSARY DECORATION ➡

2011 | 2 x 2 x 1.5 cm
Gold, black diamond, niello;
fabricated, set
Photos by artist

THE ARTISTS

ANNE ACHENBACH
Anne Achenbach was born in Marburg, Germany, in 1985. A graduate of the University of Applied Sciences in Düsseldorf, Germany, she holds a bachelor's degree in applied art and design. In 2008, Anne won a Swarovski Innovation Award. Two years later, she was awarded first prize in Young Applied Arts by the Bavarian Crafts Council. Anne has exhibited her work throughout Germany, Austria, and Netherlands. She lives in Düsseldorf.

PIA ALEBORG
Pia Aleborg is a contemporary jewelry artist based in Gothenburg, Sweden. She studied at the HDK School of Design and Crafts at the University of Gothenburg and at the Central Saint Martins College of Art and Design in London, England. Pia works with nontraditional materials to create jewelry that's innovative, distinctive, and unusual. She has exhibited her work extensively throughout Europe and the United States.

NICOLE BECK
Born in Munich, Germany, Nicole Beck began training as a goldsmith in 1999 at the State College for Glass and Jewelry in Neugablonz/Kaufbeuren, Germany. She completed her apprenticeship in 2002, then studied jewelry at Pforzheim University in Pforzheim, Germany, receiving her diploma in 2007. Nicole has participated in several exhibitions, and her work is held in the Marzee Collection in Nijmegen, Netherlands. She is currently based in Munich, where she is continuing her studies at the Munich Academy of Fine Arts.

SOFIA BJÖRKMAN
A curator and jewelry designer, Sofia Björkman lives in Stockholm, Sweden. She holds an MFA from the Konstfack University College of Arts, Crafts, and Design in Stockholm. She is the founder of Platina, a gallery in Stockholm that promotes the work of important jewelry artists. Through her own jewelry designs, Sofia poses questions about material value and status. She has exhibited her work in galleries throughout Europe and the United States.

ALLYSON BONE
Allyson Bone was born and raised in Iowa City, Iowa. She began her studies in metalsmithing and jewelry at the University of Iowa in Iowa City, where she received BAs in psychology and studio art. In 2011 she earned an MFA in metal from the State University of New York at New Paltz. Allyson is interested in jewelry as a means of mobile self-expression. Based in Brooklyn, New York, she works as a full-time jewelry designer.

BURCU BÜYÜKÜNAL
Burcu Büyükünal was born in 1980 in Ankara, Turkey. She graduated from the Industrial Design Department of Istanbul Technical University in 2003. Three years later, she received a Fulbright Award and moved to the United States to study jewelry and metalsmithing at the State University of New York at New Paltz. Burcu's work has been exhibited in shows around the world. Currently, she is a part-time jewelry design instructor at Istanbul Technical University, where she is also pursuing a PhD in art history.

SID CALDWELL
Sid Caldwell was born in Richmond, Virginia, sometime in the early 1980s. At sixteen, she began a semi-nomadic lifestyle, moving to Exeter, New Hampshire, to attend Phillips Exeter Academy. She went west for college, passing through Portland, Oregon, and San Francisco, California, before returning to Virginia. Sid holds a BFA in crafts/material studies from Virginia Commonwealth University in Richmond and an MFA in metalsmithing from the Cranbrook Academy of Art in Bloomfield Hills, Michigan. She lives in Richmond.

DAVID CHOI
David Choi received his BFA in 2009 from the University of Illinois–Urbana-Champaign and his MFA in 2011 from the State University of New York at New Paltz. He has shown his work at invitational and juried exhibitions in the United States and abroad. He lives in Chicago, Illinois.

ALICE JEE CHUNG

Alice Jee Chung graduated in 2009 from the Rhode Island School of Design with a degree in jewelry and metalsmithing. After college, she began working as a designer of fashion accessories and jewelry. Alice holds an Accredited Jewelry Professional diploma from the Gemological Institute of America. She lives in Seoul, South Korea.

THEA CLARK

A native of Spain, Thea Clark was raised in New York, New York, and San Francisco, California. She studied jewelry making at the College of Marin in Kentfield, California, and stone setting at the Revere Academy in San Francisco. Founder of the New Jersey Metal Arts Guild, Thea has exhibited her work in galleries and museums around the world. She is currently an instructor at the New Jersey Center of Visual Arts in Summit, New Jersey.

DR. TINE DE RUYSSER

Dr. Tine De Ruysser trained as a jeweler at the Royal Academy of Fine Arts in Antwerp, Belgium, and the Royal College of Art in London, England. She has exhibited her work worldwide and won several competitions, including Talente 2004, the 56th Bavarian State Prize, and the Armourers and Brasiers' Company Award for innovative work in metal. She lives in London, England.

LAURA DEAKIN

A native of Melbourne, Australia, Laura Deakin studied photography and sculpture at the Royal Melbourne Institute of Technology. She holds a BFA in contemporary jewelry from Monash University in Melbourne. In 2007 she won the Emerging Craftsperson Award from the Bavarian Art Association. She completed her postgraduate studies at the Academy of Fine Art in Munich, Germany, in 2010, the same year she received first prize in the Bavarian State Prize for Emerging Designers. Laura's work is held in the permanent collections of the Museum of Modern Art in Munich and the Galerie Marzee in Nijmegen, Netherlands. Laura lives and works in Munich.

JULIA deVILLE

Julia deVille produces jewelry under the label Disce Mori. Applying traditional gold and silversmithing techniques to materials that were once living, such as petrified wood, human hair, and taxidermy, she creates pieces inspired by Victorian mourning jewelry. A native of New Zealand, Julia has exhibited her work in Europe and the United States. She lives in Collingwood, Victoria, Australia.

CAROLINA GIMENO

Representing the third generation of a family of jewelry makers, Carolina Gimeno was born in Valparaíso, Chile, in 1981. She began designing at an early age, learning to view jewelry as a manifestation of the arts rather than a form of ornamental craft. In 2010, Carolina completed a degree in jewelry making at the Massana School in Barcelona, Spain. Based in Barcelona, she exhibits regularly throughout Europe and the United States.

STEFAN HEUSER

Stefan Heuser was born in Koblenz am Rhein, Germany, in 1978. He works with unusual substances such as breast milk, sleeping pills, and human fat removed in liposuctions to create jewelry that explores preconceived ideas about value and material. Stefan has participated in exhibits throughout Europe. A graduate of the Munich Academy of Fine Arts, he lives in Munich, Germany.

MIRJAM HILLER

Mirjam Hiller lives and works in Potsdam, Germany. She studied jewelry making and design at Pforzheim University in Pforzheim, Germany, and the Nova Scotia College of Art and Design in Halifax, Nova Scotia, Canada. Her award-winning work is included in the public collections of the Grassimuseum in Leipzig, Germany; the Middlesbrough Institute of Modern Art in Middlesbrough, England; and the Mint Museum of Art in Charlotte, North Carolina.

THE ARTISTS

BEPPE KESSLER

Beppe Kessler graduated in 1979 from the Gerrit Rietveld Academy in Amsterdam, Netherlands, where she studied textiles. From 1982 to 2005 she taught at various art institutes in Netherlands. Her work has been exhibited in museums around the world, including the Rijksmuseum in Amsterdam; the Museum of Fine Arts in Boston, Massachusetts; and the National Museum of Scotland in Edinburgh. She lives and works in Amsterdam.

SUSANNE KLEMM

Susanne Klemm was born in 1965 in Zurich, Switzerland. She was educated at the Utrecht School of the Arts in Utrecht, Netherlands, and the Zurich University of the Arts in Zurich. Susanne has participated in exhibitions throughout Europe and the United States. Her work is in the public collections of the Museum of Arts and Design in New York, New York; the Rijksmuseum in Amsterdam, Netherlands; and the Hiko Mizuno School of Jewelry in Tokyo, Japan. She lives in Amsterdam.

AGNES LARSSON

Agnes Larsson was born in Stockholm, Sweden, in 1980. She holds BFA and MFA degrees in silversmithing and jewelry from the Konstfack University College of Arts, Crafts, and Design in Stockholm. In 2010, she received the Art Jewelry Forum's Emerging Artist award. Her work has been exhibited throughout Europe and the United States. Since 2007, she has maintained a jewelry studio outside of Stockholm.

ALISSIA MELKA-TEICHROEW

Daughter of a French mother and an American father, Alissia Melka-Teichroew, founder and creative director of byAMT Studio, is a New World-Old World mash-up. She was born and raised in Netherlands. A graduate of the Design Academy Eindhoven in Eindhoven, Netherlands, she holds a master's degree in industrial design from the Rhode Island School of Design. Alissia's uncanny ability to tweak expectations has delighted design cognoscenti and consumers alike. *Nylon*, *I. D.*, and *The New York Times*, among other publications, have featured her creations. She lives and works in New York, New York.

ANDREA G. MILLER

Andrea G. Miller is a visual artist whose practice is greatly influenced by the traditions of metalsmithing. Through her work she investigates the man-made environment in relation to the human body and culture. Born and raised in the Midwest, Andrea holds an MFA from the University of Wisconsin in Madison and a BFA from Ball State University in Muncie, Indiana. Community outreach and public education through the arts are important parts of her work.

NERVOUS SYSTEM

Based in Shutesbury, Massachusetts, Nervous System consists of Jessica Rosenkrantz and Jesse Louis-Rosenberg, who met as undergraduates at the Massachusetts Institute of Technology (MIT). Jessica graduated from MIT in 2005 with degrees in architecture and biology. She went on to study architecture at the Harvard Graduate School of Design. Jesse majored in mathematics at MIT, then worked as a consultant for Gehry Technologies. The pair established Nervous System, their experimental design studio, in 2007.

SETH PAPAC

Seth Papac holds a BFA from the University of Washington in Seattle and an MFA from the Cranbrook Academy of Art in Bloomfield Hills, Michigan. His work has been exhibited internationally and can be found in the permanent collections of the Museum of Contemporary Craft in Portland, Oregon; the Cranbrook Art Museum in Bloomfield Hills, Michigan; and the Tacoma Art Museum in Tacoma, Washington. Currently an artist in residence at San Diego State University, Seth lectures throughout the United States and abroad.

NORA ROCHEL

Nora Rochel was born in Heidelberg, Germany. She studied metalwork and jewelry design at Pforzheim University in Pforzheim, Germany, and Kookmin University in Seoul, South Korea. Her award-winning work has been featured in exhibitions throughout Europe. She lives in Karlsruhe, Germany.

GASTÓN ROIS
Gastón Rois was born in Buenos Aires, Argentina, in 1975. In 1998, with no formal training, he began working as a jewelry designer. Hoping to broaden his aesthetic, he traveled to Barcelona, Spain, in 2006 to study jewelry at the Massana School. He went on to study at the Saimaa University of Applied Sciences in Imatra-Lappeenranta, Finland. Based in Barcelona, Gastón exhibits regularly in Europe and America.

LUCY SARNEEL
Lucy Sarneel is an instructor at the Gerrit Rietveld Academy in Amsterdam, Netherlands. Her work is in public collections around the world, including those of the Cooper Hewitt, National Design Museum in New York, New York; the Stedelijk Museum in Amsterdam; and the Schmuckmuseum in Pforzheim, Germany. Lucy's award-winning jewelry reflects her exploration of the tension that exists between the present and the past, nature and civilization. Her work has been featured in numerous publications and exhibited internationally.

SANNA SVEDESTEDT
The author of a popular jewelry blog, Sanna Svedestedt works for www.klimt02.net, the art-jewelry website. In 2009, after graduating with a degree in jewelry art from the HDK School of Design and Crafts at the University of Gothenburg in Gothenburg, Sweden, Sanna opened her own workshop. In addition to organizing shows and projects, she exhibits her work internationally. She lives in Gothenburg.

ROBEAN VISSCHERS
Robean Visschers was born in 1980 in Zwolle, Netherlands. He studied metalsmithing at the Vakschool Schoonhoven in Schoonhoven, Netherlands, and the Alchimia Contemporary Jewelry School in Florence, Italy, where he found a mentor in Philip Sajet. His work has been exhibited in group shows throughout Netherlands and Germany. He lives in Utrecht, Netherlands.

JOE WOOD
Joe Wood has been teaching jewelry, metalsmithing, and other classes at the Massachusetts College of Art in Boston since 1985. He has taught workshops at the Royal College of Art in London, England; the Haystack Mountain School of Crafts in Deer Isle, Maine; and the Penland School of Crafts in Penland, North Carolina. His work has been exhibited internationally and is now in the public collections of the Smithsonian American Art Museum's

Renwick Gallery in Washington, DC; the Museum of Fine Arts in Racine, Wisconsin; and the Museum of Fine Arts in Boston.

LI-CHU WU
Li-Chu Wu is a Taiwanese jewelry maker based in Birmingham, England. She studied jewelry design at Fu Jen Catholic University in New Taipei City, Taiwan, and did graduate work at Birmingham City University, where she earned a master's degree in jewelry making and silversmithing. In 2010, Li-Chu was selected for a program called Design Space, which was sponsored by the Birmingham City Council and the European Regional Development Fund and provided her with free studio space to work as an independent jewelry designer. Her work has been exhibited throughout Europe and in Portugal and Taiwan.

ABOUT THE CURATOR   INDEX

ABOUT THE CURATOR

Arthur Hash was born in Balboa, Panama, in 1976. He holds an MFA in metalsmithing and jewelry design from Indiana University and a BFA in craft/material studies from Virginia Commonwealth University. Since 2009, Arthur has worked in the metal program at the State University of New York at New Paltz. His work is included in a number of private and public collections around the United States and has been featured in numerous publications, including the magazines *Metalsmith*, *American Craft*, *Domino*, and *Niche*. Arthur's work reflects his commitment to the exploration of what jewelry is and can be even as it exhibits the sense of elegance and beauty that characterizes the long tradition of body adornment. He lives in New Paltz, New York.